Spiritual Meditations for Teenagers - Volume 1

Dianna Miller

iUniverse, Inc.
New York   Bloomington

Spiritual Meditations for Teenagers - Volume 1

iUniverse books may be ordered through booksellers or by contacting:

iUniverse
1663 Liberty Drive
Bloomington, IN 47403
www.iuniverse.com
1-800-Authors (1-800-288-4677)

Because of the dynamic nature of the Internet, any Web addresses or links contained in this
book may have changed since publication and may no longer be valid. The views expressed
in this work are solely those of the author and do not necessarily reflect the views of the
publisher, and the publisher hereby disclaims any responsibility for them.

ISBN: 978-1-4502-5369-7 (sc)
ISBN: 978-1-4502-5370-3 (ebook)

Printed in the United States of America

iUniverse rev. date: 9/28/2010

DEDICATION

I DEDICATE THIS BOOK TO:

THE HOLY SPIRIT FOR USING ME AS HIS INSTRUMENT IN DOING THESE MEDITATIONS.

MY WONDERFUL SON, CHAD, WHOSE EARTHLY LIFE ENDED ON JULY 15, 1999.

MY FAMILY AND ALL MY DEAR FRIENDS FOR THEIR SUPPORT.

FATHER FRED FOR HELPING ME FINANCE THE PUBLISHING OF THIS BOOK.

JANELLE FOR EDITING THIS BOOK FOR ME.

BARB AND CHRISTIE FOR ALLOWING ME TO DO THESE MEDITATIONS WITH THEIR SEVENTH AND EIGHTH GRADE STUDENTS.

ALL THE DEAR TEACHERS I WORKED WITH IN THE LAST THIRTY-EIGHT YEARS.

THE 2009-2010 SEVENTH AND EIGHTH GRADERS AT ST. JOSEPH SCHOOL FOR DOING THESE MEDITATIONS WITH ME AND FOR THEIR SUPPORT AND ENCOURAGEMENT.

FORWARD

IN THE LAST SEVERAL YEARS OF MY CAREER I WAS EXPOSED TO THE IDEA OF DOING MEDITATIONS WITH MY STUDENTS. I LOOKED IN RELIGIOUS STORES FOR THAT TYPE OF BOOK AND DISCOVERED THERE WERE NONE FOR TEENAGERS THAT I COULD FIND. I STARTED DOING MEDITATIONS WITH MY SIXTH GRADERS DURING MY LAST YEAR OF TEACHING, AND THEY LOVED THEM. THEY SAID THAT THE MEDITATIONS BROUGHT THEM CLOSER TO GOD. IN ORDER TO KEEP HIS SPIRIT ALIVE IN OUR STUDENTS, I DECIDED TO SPEND MY FIRST YEAR OF RETIREMENT PUTTING THESE MEDITATIONS IN A BOOK THAT COULD BE SHARED WITH ALL TEACHERS WHO TEACH TEENAGERS. THIS BOOK IS TARGETED FOR ALL CATHOLIC AND CHRISTIAN SCHOOLS.

THIS BOOK OF MEDITATIONS WAS DONE ONLY WITH THE INSPIRATION OF THE HOLY SPIRIT. BEFORE AND DURING THE WRITING OF EACH ONE I PRAYED TO HIM FOR INSPIRATION AND ALLOWED HIM TO DO HIS WORK THROUGH ME. I THANK HIM FOR ALLOWING ME TO BE HIS INSTRUMENT.

THERE IS A MEDITATION FOR EACH WEEK OF A THIRTY-SIX WEEK SCHOOL YEAR. THE FIRST MEDITATION BEGINS THE SECOND WEEK OF SEPTEMBER SINCE YOU WILL NEED THAT FIRST WEEK FOR ORIENTATION. SOME MONTHS THE MEDITATIONS ARE NUMBERED SO YOU CAN KEEP TRACK OF EACH WEEK. THE ONES FOR ADVENT AND LENT ARE NOT NUMBERED BUT THERE ARE MEDITATIONS FOR

THE FOUR WEEKS OF ADVENT AND THE SIX WEEKS OF LENT. THE MEDITATIONS FOR THE SEASON OF LENT ARE CENTERED ON THE SORROWFUL MYSTERIES. BECAUSE THE DATE OF EASTER VARIES EACH YEAR, YOU WILL HAVE TO SCHEDULE THESE MEDITATIONS AT THE APPROPRIATE TIMES.

EACH MEDITATION BEGINS WITH A SETTING SO THE STUDENTS CAN VISUALIZE AN INSPIRATIONAL PLACE. WHEN YOU COME TO THE WORD "PAUSE" PLEASE GIVE THE STUDENTS THREE TO FIVE SECONDS TO MEDITATE ON THAT SECTION.

TEACHERS: BEFORE YOU BEGIN EACH MEDITATION HAVE THE STUDENTS CLEAR THEIR DESKS OF EVERYTHING AND ASK THEM TO SIT IN SILENCE. PARENTS DOING THESE MEDITATIONS AT HOME: FIND A PLACE WITH NO DISTRACTIONS. HAVE THEM CLOSE THEIR EYES DURING THE ENTIRE MEDITATION. AT THE END OF THE MEDITATION THEY WILL SPEND A FEW MOMENTS IN SILENT PRAYER. LET EACH STUDENT OPEN THEIR EYES WHEN THEY ARE READY. WHEN ALL STUDENTS HAVE OPENED THEIR EYES, PROCEED WITH THE DISCUSSION GUIDE.

THE DISCUSSION GUIDE AFTER EACH MEDITATION HELPS THE STUDENTS SEE HOW THEY CAN APPLY THE MESSAGE TO THEIR DAILY LIVES AND TO KNOW THEY ARE NOT ALONE IN THEIR JOURNEY.

IT IS RECOMMENDED THAT THE MEDITATIONS BE DONE ONCE A WEEK IN ORDER TO HAVE THE GREATEST IMPACT ON THE STUDENTS. GOD BLESS EACH OF YOU FOR SPREADING HIS WORD AND HIS LOVE.

(ANY FEEDBACK WOULD BE GREATLY APPRECIATED. PLEASE FORWARD YOUR COMMENTS TO: dmiller4746@bex. net.)

Table of Contents

HANNAH'S TESTIMONIAL LETTER

(ON THE NIGHT OF THE EIGHTH GRADE GRADUATION AN EIGHTH GRADE STUDENT GAVE ME THIS LETTER.)

MS. MILLER,

I'VE NEVER WRITTEN A LETTER TO A TEACHER BEFORE, BUT SINCE YOU ARE NO LONGER ONE OF MY GRADE SCHOOL TEACHERS, I DECIDED IT WAS OKAY. YOU STILL TEACH ME RELIGION AND VALUES, SOME OF WHICH ARE SO NEW TO ME. I CAN NEVER TELL YOU HOW MUCH YOU HAVE CHANGED MY LIFE. YOU HAVE EMBRACED GOD'S MESSAGE AND HAVE REALLY MEANT A LOT TO ME. I WAS SAD TO SEE YOU GO FROM TEACHING. I MISS SO MUCH SEEING YOUR SMILE AND LOVE EVERYDAY. YOU REALLY CARED ABOUT THE STUDENTS. I THANK GOD THAT HE HAS GIVEN ME SOMEONE LIKE YOU.

I STILL CAN'T THANK YOU ENOUGH. YOU WILL NEVER KNOW HOW MUCH YOU HAVE CHANGED MY WAY OF THINKING. I FEEL CLOSER TO GOD NOW, AND IT IS ALL BECAUSE OF YOU. YOU HAVE HELPED ME PRAY AND ANSWER MY QUESTIONS. I WILL MISS YOUR MEDITATIONS, BUT I LOOK FORWARD TO YOUR BOOK. PLEASE CONTINUE TO HELP KIDS GROW IN THEIR FAITH. THEY WILL BE SO GRATEFUL. I'M GOING TO STOP NOW BECAUSE I AM CRYING SO HARD. SORRY THIS WAS MESSY, BUT TEARS ARE HARD TO SEE THROUGH. I WILL NEVER FORGET YOU, MS. MILLER. YOU HAVE TRULY BEEN A DISCIPLE OF CHRIST.

LOVE,

HANNAH

SEPTEMBER: WEEK 1 - THE BEGINNING OF A NEW SCHOOL YEAR

CLOSE YOUR EYES.

BREATHE IN DEEPLY, HOLD IT, BREATHE OUT. (3 TIMES)

PICTURE YOURSELF IN A GARDEN OF FLOWERS: RED, ORANGE, AND YELLOW. THERE IS A BENCH NEARBY, AND YOU SIT DOWN AND RELAX.

YOU ARE THINKING ABOUT THE BEGINNING OF A NEW SCHOOL YEAR AND BEING IN A NEW GRADE. (PAUSE)

WHAT WILL IT BE LIKE? (PAUSE)

WILL I BE ABLE TO DO ALL THE WORK ASKED OF ME? (PAUSE)

WILL I MAKE NEW FRIENDS? (PAUSE)

AS YOU ARE WONDERING ALL THESE THINGS, A STRANGER SITS DOWN BESIDE YOU. HE SAYS, "I KNOW ALL THE QUESTIONS IN YOUR MIND. LET ME ANSWER THEM FOR YOU.

"FIRST OF ALL, YOUR NEW YEAR WILL BE FULL OF NEW EXPERIENCES AND NEW KNOWLEDGE ABOUT YOURSELF, YOUR WORLD, AND ME. (PAUSE)

"SECONDLY, IF YOU PUT ALL YOUR EFFORT INTO YOUR STUDIES YOU WILL BE ABLE TO DO THE WORK. IF YOU STRUGGLE THERE WILL BE HELP FOR YOU. (PAUSE)

"YOU ASKED IF YOU WOULD MAKE NEW FRIENDS. YES, YOU WILL AND I HOPE THAT I AM AT THE TOP OF YOUR LIST." (PAUSE)

"WHO ARE YOU?" YOU ASK.

"I AM YOUR BEST FRIEND, JESUS. I SO MUCH WANT YOU TO GET TO KNOW ME AND KNOW THAT I WILL ALWAYS TAKE CARE OF YOU. (PAUSE) ALL I ASK IN RETURN IS THAT YOU WILL SHARE YOUR LOVE WITH ALL THOSE YOU MEET EACH DAY. SOMETIMES A SMILE ALONE CAN MEAN A LOT. (PAUSE)

"RESPECT YOUR TEACHERS AND FELLOW STUDENTS. GIVE THEM A HELPING HAND WHEN THEY NEED IT. (PAUSE)

I AM CALLING YOU TO BE ME TODAY IN YOUR SMALL WORLD. MAKE A DIFFEERENCE. (PAUSE)

"I MUST GO NOW, BUT KNOW THAT I AM ALWAYS WITH YOU. HAVE A GREAT SCHOOL YEAR! I LOVE YOU DEARLY."

(SPEND A FEW MOMENTS IN SILENT PRAYER.)

DISCUSSION GUIDE

1. WHAT ARE YOUR GOALS FOR THIS NEW SCHOOL YEAR?

2. WHAT ARE SOME WAYS THAT YOU CAN MAKE THE YEAR A GOOD ONE?

    1. FOR YOURSELF?

    2. FOR YOUR PARENTS?

    3. FOR YOUR TEACHER(S)?

    4. FOR YOUR CLASSMATES?

3. WHAT COULD YOU DO TO BE A GOOD LEADER IN YOUR CLASS?

4. WHAT COULD YOU DO TO BE A GOOD CHRISTIAN?

SEPTEMBER: WEEK 2 - TRIP TO THE ZOO WITH JESUS

CLOSE YOUR EYES

BREATHE IN DEEPLY, HOLD IT, BREATHE OUT. (3 TIMES)

YOU ARE GOING WITH JESUS ON A TRIP TO THE ZOO. (PAUSE)

YOU SEE THE LIONS AND TIGERS AND THINK ABOUT THE TREMENDOUS STRENGTH AND POWER THEY HAVE. JESUS SAYS, "WHEN YOU SEE THESE ANIMALS, I WANT YOU TO REMEMBER THE TREMENDOUS POWER THAT I HAVE GIVEN YOU. THE POWER TO LAUGH (PAUSE), THE POWER TO CRY OVER INJUSTICE IN THIS WORLD (PAUSE), AND THE POWER TO LOVE DEEPLY." (PAUSE)

YOU SEE THE MONKEYS AND ALL THE THINGS THEY DO TO MAKE YOU LAUGH. (PAUSE) JESUS SAYS, "WHEN YOU SEE THESE ANIMALS I WANT YOU TO REMEMBER THE GIFT OF LAUGHTER THAT I HAVE GIVEN YOU. ENJOY THIS GIFT WITH YOUR FAMILY, YOUR FRIENDS, YOUR CLASSMATES, AND YOUR TEACHERS." (PAUSE)

YOU WALK OVER AND SEE THE ELEPHANTS. ONE IS SPRAYING WATER ON HIMSELF. JESUS SAYS, "JUST LIKE THE ELEPHANT IS SHOWERING HIMSELF, I WANT YOU TO REMEMBER ALL THE GRACES I SHOWER ON YOU: THE

GRACE TO OVERCOME TEMPTATIONS (PAUSE), THE GRACE TO FORGIVE OTHERS (PAUSE), AND THE GRACE TO LEARN FROM YOUR FAILURES." (PAUSE)

YOU NOW SEE THE CAMELS AND THE BIG HUMPS ON THEIR BACKS. JESUS SAYS, "DO YOU SEE HOW THEY CARRY THE EXTRA WEIGHT ON THEIR BACKS? LET THIS REMIND YOU OF ALL THE CROSSES I ASK YOU TO CARRY: THE CROSS OF SCHOOLWORK, THE CROSS OF LOSING A LOVED ONE, THE CROSS OF SICKNESS. (PAUSE) CARRY THESE CROSSES WITH LOVE IN YOUR HEART, JUST AS I CARRIED MINE OUT OF MY LOVE FOR YOU." (PAUSE)

THE LAST ANIMALS YOU SEE ARE THE BEAUTIFUL VARIETY OF BIRDS.

JESUS SAYS, "JUST AS I HAVE GIVEN THESE BIRDS WINGS TO FLY, SO I GIVE YOU WINGS TO FLY: WINGS TO ENJOY THE GIFT OF LIFE I HAVE GIVEN YOU, (PAUSE) WINGS TO USE THE GIFTS I HAVE GIVEN YOU TO MAKE A DIFFERENCE IN THE WORLD, (PAUSE) AND IN THE END, WINGS TO FLY HOME TO ME." (PAUSE)

(SPEND A FEW MOMENTS IN SILENT PRAYER.)

DISCUSSION GUIDE

1. NAME SOME WAYS GOD BESTOWS GRACE UPON YOU EACH DAY.

2. WHAT ARE SOME INJUSTICES IN OUR WORLD TODAY?

3. WHAT ARE SOME OF THE CROSSES GOD MIGHT ASK YOU TO CARRY THIS YEAR?

4. NAME SOME WAYS YOU CAN SHARE YOUR GIFTS AND TALENTS THIS YEAR.

SEPTEMBER: WEEK 3 - MEDITATION ON THE POOR

CLOSE YOUR EYES.

BREATHE IN DEEPLY, HOLD IT, BREATHE OUT. (3 TIMES)

JESUS ASKS YOU TO TAKE A WALK WITH HIM DOWN A DIRT ROAD IN A VERY POOR COUNTRY. (PAUSE) HE POINTS OUT A CARDBOARD SHACK IN WHICH PEOPLE ARE LIVING. (PAUSE) THEY HAVE NO RUNNING WATER, NO HEAT FOR THE COLD WINTERS, AND NO AIR CONDITIONING FOR THE HOT SUMMERS. (PAUSE) THEY WONDER EACH DAY IF THEY WILL HAVE ANYTHING AT ALL TO EAT. (PAUSE) MOST NIGHTS THEY GO TO BED HUNGRY. (PAUSE) YOU LOOK AT JESUS AND THANK HIM WITH ALL YOUR HEART THAT YOU ARE SO BLESSED TO HAVE THE THINGS THEY DON'T HAVE. (PAUSE) JESUS SAYS, "WHEN YOU SEE ME HOMELESS, GIVE ME SHELTER. (PAUSE) WHEN YOU SEE ME NAKED, GIVE ME CLOTHING. (PAUSE) WHEN YOU SEE ME HUNGRY, GIVE ME FOOD. (PAUSE) WHEN YOU SEE ME THIRSTY, GIVE ME DRINK. (PAUSE) WHATEVER YOU DO TO OTHERS, YOU DO UNTO ME." (PAUSE)

YOU ASK JESUS, "WHEN DID I SEE YOU HUNGRY, THIRSTY, OR NAKED?"

JESUS SAYS, "WHEN YOU SHARED YOUR LUNCH WITH A FELLOW CLASSMATE, YOU WERE FEEDING ME. (PAUSE) WHEN YOU GAVE SOMEONE A DRINK, YOU QUENCHED MY THIRST. (PAUSE) WHEN YOU DONATED YOUR CLOTHING, YOU CLOTHED ME. (PAUSE) WHEN YOU VISITED THE LONELY, YOU WERE VISITING ME. (PAUSE) I HAVE SENT YOU INTO THE WORLD TO BE ME TO OTHERS. TELL THEM OF MY GREAT LOVE FOR THEM. (PAUSE) SHOW THEM WHAT A FOLLOWER OF CHRIST DOES."

YOU ASK JESUS, "PLEASE GIVE ME THE GRACE TO BE YOU IN THIS WORLD, TO BRING COMPASSION TO THOSE THAT ARE IN TEARS, (PAUSE) UNDERSTANDING TO THOSE WHO ARE HURTING, (PAUSE) LOVE TO THOSE WHO NEED IT, A HUG FOR THOSE WHO ARE SAD, (PAUSE) HELP TO THOSE WHO ARE STRUGGLING, (PAUSE) AND YOUR LIGHT TO THOSE WHO ARE IN THE DARKNESS OF SIN. (PAUSE) HELP ME MAKE THE WORLD A BETTER PLACE BY BEING YOU TODAY."

(SPEND A FEW MOMENTS IN SILENT PRAYER)

DISCUSSION GUIDE

1. GIVE SOME EXAMPLES OF HOW YOU CAN HELP THE HOMELESS.

2. HOW MIGHT YOU HELP CLOTHE THE NAKED?

3. HOW MIGHT YOU BE ABLE TO HELP THE HUNGRY?

4. GIVE SOME EXAMPLES OF TIMES WHEN YOU COULD GIVE DRINK TO THOSE THAT ARE THIRSTY.

OCTOBER: WEEK 1 - OUR BLESSED MOTHER

CLOSE YOUR EYES.

BREATHE IN DEEPLY, HOLD IT, BREATHE OUT. (3 TIMES)

OCTOBER IS A MONTH IN WHICH THE CATHOLIC CHURCH HONORS OUR BLESSED MOTHER, MARY.

JESUS INVITES YOU TODAY TO MEET THIS VERY SPECIAL PERSON, HIS MOTHER. HE ASKS YOU TO LOOK AT HER AND SEE WHAT HE SEES -- THE LOOK OF A MOTHER'S LOVE ON HER FACE. (PAUSE)

JESUS SAYS, "SHE ANSWERED THE CALL OF BEING MY MOTHER SO THAT YOU COULD BE WITH ME IN HEAVEN. (PAUSE) SHE GAVE BIRTH TO ME JUST AS YOUR MOTHER GAVE BIRTH TO YOU. SHE HELD ME IN HER ARMS JUST AS YOUR MOTHER HOLDS YOU. (PAUSE) SHE DRIED AWAY MY TEARS JUST AS YOUR MOTHER DRIES YOURS. (PAUSE) WE LAUGHED TOGETHER AND HAD FUN TOGETHER. I WANT TO SHARE MY MOTHER WITH YOU. PLEASE LISTEN TO WHAT SHE HAS TO SAY TO YOU TODAY."

MARY SAYS, "I AM YOUR MOTHER TOO, AND I LOVE YOU IN THE SAME WAY I LOVE MY SON, JESUS. I WILL LISTEN TO YOUR PRAYERS AND ASK HIM TO ANSWER THEM. I WILL HOLD YOU IN MY ARMS WHEN YOU NEED

A HUG. MY SON AND I WILL BE AT YOUR SIDE ALWAYS TO GUIDE YOU ALONG THE WAY OF LIFE. I ENCOURAGE YOU TO LISTEN TO HIS WORDS BECAUSE HE IS THE WAY, THE TRUTH, AND THE LIFE. (PAUSE) WITHOUT HIM IN YOUR LIFE YOU WILL FEEL EMPTY AND LIFE WILL HAVE NO MEANING. BUT WITH HIM IN YOUR LIFE YOU WILL EXPERIENCE REAL PEACE, HAPPINESS AND JOY. I KNOW I DO. (PAUSE) I WATCHED MY SON GIVE UP HIS LIFE ON THE CROSS SO THAT YOU COULD BE WITH HIM IN HEAVEN. HE LOVES YOU THAT MUCH." (PAUSE)

MARY SAYS TO JESUS, "PLEASE WATCH OVER THESE WONDERFUL CHILDREN. GIVE THEM THE COURAGE TO OVERCOME TEMPTATIONS AND DO WHAT IS RIGHT. (PAUSE) GIVE THEM THE GRACE TO ENJOY THE LIFE YOU HAVE GIVEN THEM AND, AT THE SAME TIME, TO ALWAYS DO YOUR WILL. (PAUSE) IGNITE THEM WITH THE FIRE OF YOUR LOVE AND LET THEIR HEARTS BURN WITH THE DESIRE TO SERVE YOU AND BE YOU IN THE WORLD." (PAUSE)

(SPEND A FEW MOMENTS IN SILENT PRAYER.)

DISCUSSION GUIDE

1. NAME SOME WAYS THAT YOUR MOTHER IS LIKE MARY.

2. HOW DID JESUS TREAT HIS MOTHER?

3. WHAT ARE SOME PRAYERS YOU CAN SAY TO OUR BLESSED MOTHER?

   HERE ARE A FEW PRAYERS TO OUR LADY:

   ---THE HAIL MARY

   ---CONSECRATION TO MARY

   ---THE MEMORARE

4. NAME SOME WAYS YOU CAN IMITATE OUR BLESSED MOTHER.

OCTOBER: WEEK 2 - THE PURPOSE OF LIFE

CLOSE YOUR EYES.

BREATHE IN, HOLD IT, BREATHE OUT (3 TIMES)

YOU AND JESUS ARE WALKING HAND IN HAND ON A WHITE SANDY BEACH. YOU FEEL THE SUN AND THE WARM BREEZE ON YOUR FACE. (PAUSE) YOU ASK JESUS, "WHY DID YOU PUT ME HERE ON EARTH? IS THERE SOMETHING SPECIAL YOU WANT ME TO DO WITH THE LIFE YOU HAVE GIVEN ME?" (PAUSE)

JESUS SAYS TO YOU, "I PUT YOU ON THIS EARTH TO TAKE MY PLACE AND TO MAKE A DIFFERENCE JUST AS I DID. (PAUSE) I DO HAVE THINGS I WANT YOU TO DO IN YOUR LIFETIME. RIGHT NOW I WANT YOU TO BE THE BEST STUDENT YOU CAN BE AND TO DEVELOP THE TALENTS I HAVE GIVEN YOU. (PAUSE) NO MATTER WHAT YOU DO IN YOUR LIFE ALWAYS REMEMBER TO LOVE OTHERS FIRST. PRAY TO ME FOR THE GUIDANCE IN DISCOVERING YOUR GIFTS. (PAUSE) IF YOU LOVE DOING CERTAIN THINGS THEN THOSE ARE THE GIFTS I HAVE GIVEN YOU. PERHAPS YOU LOVE MUSIC. DEVELOP THAT GIFT AND BRING THE JOY OF MUSIC TO OTHERS. (PAUSE) PERHAPS YOU LOVE MATH. DEVELOP THAT GIFT AND BECOME A GREAT MATH TEACHER. PERHAPS YOU ENJOY TAKING CARE OF THE SICK. IF SO, THEN BE THE BEST NURSE

YOU CAN BE. REMEMBER TO DO WHAT YOU ARE GOOD AT AND WHAT YOU ENJOY THE MOST. (PAUSE) USE THE GIFTS I HAVE GIVEN YOU TO BRING MY LOVE AND JOY TO OTHERS. (PAUSE) BE THERE FOR ME. ONLY THEN WILL YOU BE LIVING YOUR LIFE TO THE FULLEST WITH PEACE, HAPPINESS, AND JOY IN YOUR HEART. (PAUSE)

DOING MY FATHER'S WILL WAS THE MOST IMPORTANT THING FOR ME IN MY LIFE ON EARTH. I WANT THAT TO BE THE MOST IMPORTANT THING FOR YOU, TOO. (PAUSE) OUR FATHER ALWAYS KNOWS WHAT IS BEST FOR US. HE HAS GIVEN YOU YOUR PARENTS AND TEACHERS TO HELP GUIDE YOU IN PREPARING FOR THE LIFE HE WANTS YOU TO LIVE. (PAUSE) LISTEN TO THEM AND LET THEM DO THE WORK I HAVE GIVEN THEM. (PAUSE) YOU GO OUT THERE IN YOUR WORLD TODAY AND MAKE A DIFFERENCE IN THE LIVES OF OTHERS YOU MEET."

YOU SAY, "THANK YOU, DEAR JESUS, FOR YOUR WORDS OF ENLIGHTENMENT. HELP ME TO DO YOUR FATHER'S WILL TODAY AND EVERY DAY. HELP ME TO BE YOU TODAY BY MAKING A DIFFERENCE."

JESUS SAYS, "I LOVE YOU, MY CHILD, AND WILL ALWAYS BE WITH YOU."

(SPEND A FEW MOMENTS IN SILENT PRAYER.)

DISCUSSION GUIDE

1. ASK STUDENTS WHAT THEY THINK ARE THE SPECIAL TALENTS GOD HAS GIVEN THEM.

2. WHAT DO YOU THINK IS GOD'S SPECIAL PURPOSE FOR YOUR LIFE?

3. HOW CAN YOU DO GOD'S WILL RIGHT NOW IN YOUR LIFE?

4. HOW CAN YOU MAKE A DIFFERENCE IN OTHER PEOPLE'S LIVES TODAY?

OCTOBER: WEEK 3 - WHY GOD GIVES US CROSSES TO CARRY

CLOSE YOUR EYES.

BREATHE IN, HOLD IT, BREATHE OUT (3 TIMES)

YOU AND JESUS ARE STANDING ON THE HILL OF CALVARY LOOKING AT THE CROSS ON WHICH HE DIED FOR US. (PAUSE) YOU ASK JESUS, "WHY DID YOU DO IT?"

JESUS ANSWERS, "I DID IT BECAUSE I LOVE YOU AND I WANT YOU TO BE IN HEAVEN WITH ME AND BECAUSE IT WAS MY HEAVENLY FATHER'S WILL." (PAUSE) JESUS SAYS TO YOU, "I WILL GIVE YOU CROSSES TO CARRY THROUGHOUT YOUR LIFE, TOO. NOT BECAUSE I WANT TO SEE YOU SUFFER, BUT BECAUSE I WANT TO SEE YOU GROW SPIRITUALLY. (PAUSE)

YOU LOOK AT HIM AND SAY, "I DON'T UNDERSTAND WHAT YOU MEAN, DEAR JESUS."

HE SAYS, "WHEN I GIVE YOU CROSSES TO BEAR, YOU HAVE TWO CHOICES. YOU CAN CHOOSE TO BE BITTER AND ANGRY AT ME OR YOU CAN ACCEPT THE CROSS AND HAVE FAITH IN ME THAT I WILL HELP YOU BECOME A BETTER PERSON FOR CARRYING IT. (PAUSE) I WILL NEVER GIVE YOU ANY CROSS THAT IS TOO HEAVY FOR YOU TO

CARRY. I WILL GIVE YOU THE STRENGTH AND COURAGE THAT YOU WILL NEED. (PAUSE)

"A CROSS THAT YOU MIGHT HAVE TO CARRY IS THE DEATH OF A LOVED ONE. (PAUSE) TREASURE THE MEMORIES YOU HAVE OF THAT PERSON AND NEVER FORGET THEM. KNOW THAT THEY ARE IN HEAVEN WITH ME AND THAT SOMEDAY YOU WILL BE WITH THEM ETERNALLY. (PAUSE) ANOTHER CROSS MAY BE THAT YOUR PARENTS DIVORCE. IF YOU DO EXPERIENCE THIS, JUST REMEMBER THEY STILL LOVE YOU, AND IT IS NOT YOUR FAULT THAT THEY CAN NO LONGER LIVE TOGETHER IN PEACE AND HARMONY. (PAUSE) YOU MAY BE CARRYING THE CROSS OF A FRIEND BEING MAD AT YOU. INVITE YOUR FRIEND TO TALK THINGS OVER. A TRUE FRIEND WILL. AND ALWAYS REMEMBER - NEVER LET THE SUN SET ON YOUR ANGER. (PAUSE) ALWAYS BE READY TO FORGIVE THOSE THAT HURT YOU, JUST AS I FORGAVE THOSE WHO CRUCIFIED ME. MY DEAR CHILD, KNOW THAT I AM ALWAYS THERE WITH YOU IN GOOD TIMES AND IN TOUGH TIMES. I WILL NEVER ABANDON YOU." (PAUSE)

YOU LOOK AT JESUS AND SAY, "DEAR JESUS, PLEASE HELP ME TO ACCEPT WHATEVER YOU HAVE PLANNED FOR ME IN MY LIFE. LET ME GROW CLOSER TO YOU BY CARRYING THE CROSSES YOU SEND ME. PLEASE LET MY FAITH IN YOU GROW DEEPER EACH DAY. I LOVE YOU AND WANT TO BE LIKE YOU IN ALL I SAY AND DO. I WISH NO MORE THAN THIS, O LORD."

JESUS GIVES YOU A BIG HUG AND SAYS, "GO IN PEACE, MY CHILD."

(SPEND A FEW MOMENTS IN SILENT PRAYER.)

DISCUSSION GUIDE

1. WOULD ANYONE LIKE TO SHARE A MEMORY OF A LOVED ONE YOU LOST?

2. WHAT DO YOU THINK IT MEANS TO "NEVER LET THE SUN SET ON YOUR ANGER?"

3. WHAT ARE SOME PROBLEMS YOU HAVE WITH YOUR FRIENDS?

4. GIVE EXAMPLES OF HOW YOU CAN FORGIVE THOSE THAT HAVE HURT YOU.

5. HOW CAN CROSSES MAKE YOU A BITTER PERSON?

6. HOW CAN CROSSES MAKE YOU A BETTER PERSON?

OCTOBER: WEEK 4 - AN AUTUMN WALK WITH JESUS

CLOSE YOUR EYES.

BREATHE IN, HOLD IT, BREATHE OUT. (3 TIMES)

YOU AND JESUS ARE WALKING ON A PATH IN THE WOODS ON A BEAUTIFUL AUTUMN DAY. JESUS TELLS YOU TO LOOK AT THE LEAVES ON THE TREES. THEY ARE BRIGHT RED, ORANGE, AND YELLOW. (PAUSE)

JESUS SAYS, "WHEN YOU SEE THE RED ONES, LET IT REMIND YOU OF THE BLOOD I SHED FOR YOU AND FOR OTHERS. (PAUSE) I HAVE GIVEN YOU MY PRECIOUS BLOOD TO DRINK SO THAT YOU WILL BE FILLED WITH MY LOVE. (PAUSE) BECAUSE OF THE BLOOD I SHED FOR YOU, YOU WILL BE WITH ME FOREVER IN HEAVEN. AT THAT TIME I WILL CALL YOU BY NAME AND WELCOME YOU INTO MY FATHER'S HOME -- A HOME OF PEACE, HAPPINESS, AND JOY."

YOU LOOK AT JESUS AND SAY, "THANK YOU, DEAR LORD, FOR THE BEST GIFT I HAVE EVER RECEIVED, YOUR LOVE.

JESUS SAYS, "WHEN YOU SEE THE ORANGE LEAVES, THINK ABOUT THE BURNING LOVE I HAVE FOR YOU. I LOVE YOU EVERY MOMENT OF EVERY DAY. I LOVE YOU WHEN YOU

ARE AWAKE. I LOVE YOU WHEN YOU ARE SLEEPING. I LOVE YOU EVEN WHEN YOU TURN AWAY FROM ME. I LOVE YOU WHEN YOU COME BACK TO ME. (PAUSE) MY LOVE IS UNCONDITIONAL. THERE IS NOTHING YOU CAN DO TO STOP ME FROM LOVING YOU. YOU CANNOT EARN MY LOVE BECAUSE IT IS ALWAYS THERE FOR YOU." (PAUSE)

YOU LOOK AT JESUS AND SAY, "THANK YOU, DEAR LORD, FOR LOVING ME AND MAKING ME YOUR CHILD FOREVER."

JESUS SAYS, "WHEN YOU SEE THE YELLOW LEAVES, THINK OF CAUTION--CAUTION IN DEALING WITH TEMPTATIONS. THERE WILL BE TIMES YOU HAVE TO CHOOSE BETWEEN SIN AND ME. THIS IS WHEN YOU HAVE TO BE CAUTIOUS. CHOOSING MY WAY OF LIFE WILL ALLOW YOU TO BE FREE OF SIN. MY WAY WILL BRING YOU HAPPINESS. SIN WILL BRING YOU SADNESS. WHICH ONE DO YOU WANT?" (PAUSE)

YOU LOOK AT JESUS AND SAY, "LORD, IT IS YOU I WANT TO FOLLOW. PLEASE GIVE ME THE GRACE TO ALWAYS CHOOSE YOU."

JESUS LOOKS INTO YOUR EYES AND SAYS, "I WILL. YOU CAN ALWAYS COUNT ON THAT."

(SPEND A FEW MOMENTS IN SILENT PRAYER.)

DISCUSSION GUIDE

1. HOW CAN YOU RESIST TEMPTAIONS?

2. WHAT DOES UNCONDITIONAL LOVE MEAN TO YOU?

3. WHAT DO YOU THINK HEAVEN IS LIKE?

4. HOW DOES IT MAKE YOU FEEL THAT GOD WILL CALL
   YOU BY NAME WHEN YOU MEET HIM IN HEAVEN?

NOVEMBER: WEEK 1 - THANKSGIVING FOR THE GIFT OF LIFE

CLOSE YOUR EYES.

BREATHE IN, HOLD IT, BREATHE OUT. (3 TIMES)

PICTURE YOURSELF AND JESUS SITTING TOGETHER IN A CHURCH. HE ASKS, "DO YOU UNDERSTAND HOW PRECIOUS THE GIFT OF YOUR LIFE IS? I HAVE CREATED BILLIONS OF LIVES SINCE THE BEGINNING OF TIME AND YOU ARE ONE OF THOSE LIVES I HAVE CHOSEN TO CREATE. (PAUSE) AT THE TIME OF YOUR CONCEPTION YOU WERE ONE CELL ONLY. IN YOUR MOTHER'S WOMB YOU GREW INTO THE CHILD I HAD DESTINED YOU TO BE FROM ALL ETERNITY. (PAUSE) NO ONE ELSE IN THE WORLD IS LIKE YOU AND NO ONE EVER WILL BE. (PAUSE)

"I WANT YOU TO ENJOY THE LIFE I HAVE GIVEN YOU, AND I WANT YOU TO LIVE EACH DAY TO THE FULLEST WITH PEACE, HAPPINESS, AND JOY IN YOUR HEART. I WANT YOU TO SHARE YOUR LIFE WITH ME. (PAUSE) SET ASIDE TIME EACH DAY TO SPEND WITH ME IN PRAYER. TELL ME ABOUT ANY CONCERNS YOU HAVE AND I WILL TAKE CARE OF THEM. SHARE WITH ME YOUR JOYS AND SORROWS, AND I WILL SMILE WITH YOU OR CRY WITH YOU. (PAUSE)

"I WANT YOU TO KNOW YOU ARE NEVER ALONE. I WILL ALWAYS BE WITH YOU. I HAVE GIVEN YOU THE GIFT OF MYSELF IN THE EUCHARIST. CAN YOU GIVE ME YOURSELF?"

YOU LOOK AT JESUS AND RESPOND, "YES, LORD, I CAN. I TRUST IN YOUR LOVE FOR ME AND KNOW THAT YOU ARE ALWAYS AT MY SIDE. I WANT TO LIVE MY LIFE FOR YOU AND WITH YOU. (PAUSE) I WANT TO THANK YOU FOR THE PRECIOUS GIFT OF MY LIFE AND MY DEEP FAITH IN YOU. I PRAY THAT MY FAITH WILL GROW DEEPER EVERY DAY. (PAUSE) ONLY WITH YOU IN MY LIFE CAN I FIND TRUE PEACE AND HAPPINESS. ST. AUGUSTINE SAID, 'OUR HEARTS ARE RESTLESS UNTIL THEY REST IN YOU, DEAR LORD.' MAY MY SOUL ALWAYS REST IN YOU AND YOU ONLY. (PAUSE)

"LORD, YOU HAVE ENTRUSTED ME TO CONTINUE THE WORK YOU BEGAN HERE ON EARTH. I PRAY, DEAR LORD, THAT I WILL BE YOUR FAITHFUL SERVANT ALWAYS."

JESUS LAYS HIS HAND ON YOUR HEAD AND BLESSES YOU. HE SAYS, "I LOVE YOU MY CHILD. I ALWAYS HAVE AND ALWAYS WILL. GO AND BE MY FAITHFUL SERVANT IN THE WORLD."

(SPEND A FEW MOMENTS IN SILENT PRAYER.)

DISCUSSION GUIDE

1. WHY DO YOU THINK GOD MADE US ALL DIFFERENT?

2. DO YOU THINK GOD WANTS US TO BE HAPPY IN THIS LIFE?

3. IN WHAT WAYS DO WE LIVE OUR LIVES FOR GOD?

4. HOW DO WE SHARE OUR LIFE WITH GOD?

NOVEMBER: WEEK 2 - THANKSGIVING FOR THE GIFT OF FAITH

CLOSE YOUR EYES.

BREATHE IN, HOLD IT, BREATHE OUT. (3 TIMES)

YOU AND JESUS ARE IN A WARM ROOM WITH VERY BRIGHT, COLORFUL LIGHTS. (PAUSE) JESUS ASKS YOU, "DO YOU KNOW WHAT THE WORD 'FAITH' MEANS? IT MEANS BELIEVING IN SOMETHING YOU CAN'T SEE. I TOLD MY APOSTLE, THOMAS, 'BLESSED ARE THOSE WHO DO NOT SEE AND BELIEVE.' THIS GIFT IS THE KEY TO HAPPINESS. (PAUSE) TO BELIEVE IN ME, YOU MUST COME TO KNOW ME, ACCEPT ME IN YOUR LIFE, AND LOVE ME." (PAUSE)

YOU ASK JESUS, "HOW DO I GET TO KNOW YOU?"

JESUS ANSWERS, "YOU WILL COME TO KNOW ME BY READING SACRED SCRIPTURE, BY DAILY PRAYER TIME WITH ME, BY LIVING YOUR LIFE ACCORDING TO THE TWO GREATEST COMMANDMENTS I GAVE YOU: TO LOVE ME ABOVE ALL ELSE AND YOUR NEIGHBOR AS YOURSELF. AND BY PARTICIPATING IN THE CELEBRATION OF THE EUCHARIST AND OTHER SACRAMENTS. THE MORE YOU GET TO KNOW ME THE MORE YOU WILL LOVE ME.

"IN SCRIPTURE YOU WILL DISCOVER THE TREMENDOUS LOVE I HAVE FOR YOU AND ALL MY CREATURES. I CURED THE SICK AND BLIND, FORGAVE SINNERS, AND BROUGHT HOPE TO THE HOPELESS. IN THE END, I GAVE MY LIFE FOR YOU. (PAUSE) I WANT TO BE YOUR BEST FRIEND FOREVER."

YOU RESPOND, "I WISH NO MORE THAT, DEAR LORD. I NEED YOU AND WANT YOU IN MY LIFE MORE THAN ANYTHING ELSE ON THIS EARTH. I LONG TO BE WITH YOU FOR ALL ETERNITY."

JESUS SAYS, "ONCE YOU GET TO KNOW ME, ACCEPT ME, AND LOVE ME, THERE WILL BE NO TURNING BACK. YOU WILL NOT WANT TO LOSE THE TREMENDOUS JOY THAT WILL BE YOURS. (PAUSE) I WANT YOU TO INVITE OTHERS TO LEARN ABOUT ME SO THEY CAN ACCEPT ME AND LOVE ME. WHEN YOU DO THIS, YOU WILL LIVE YOUR LIFE WITH PEACE, HAPPINESS, AND JOY IN YOUR HEART. THIS IS YOUR PURPOSE IN LIFE : TO BE MY INSTRUMENT OF LOVE, A LIGHT TO THE WORLD, A JOYOUS CHRISTIAN!" (PAUSE).

YOU RESPOND, "THANK YOU, DEAR LORD, FOR THE GIFT OF MY FAITH IN YOU. MAY IT GROW DEEPER EACH DAY. PLEASE HELP ME BRING OTHERS CLOSER TO YOU BY BEING THE BEST CHRISTIAN I CAN POSSIBLY BE. THANK YOU FOR THIS TIME TOGETHER. I LOVE YOU, DEAR JESUS."

JESUS SAYS, "I LOVE YOU, MY DEAR CHILD, MORE THAN YOU CAN EVER KNOW. NOW GO IN PEACE TO LOVE AND SERVE ME."

(SPEND A FEW MOMENTS IN SILENT PRAYER.)

DISCUSSION GUIDE

1. IN WHAT WAYS DO WE GET TO KNOW GOD?

2. IN WHAT WAYS CAN WE SPREAD THE FAITH?

3. HOW MANY OF YOU ENJOY SHARING YOUR FAITH WITH OTHERS?

4. HOW CAN WE DEEPEN OUR FAITH IN GOD?

NOVEMBER: WEEK 3 - THANKSGIVING FOR OUR FAMILY

CLOSE YOUR EYES.

BREATHE IN, HOLD IT, BREATHE OUT. (3 TIMES)

YOU AND JESUS ARE SITTING ON A COMFORTABLE COUCH IN YOUR HOME. JESUS INVITES YOU TO THINK ABOUT YOUR FAMILY -- YOUR MOTHER, YOUR FATHER, AND BROTHERS AND SISTERS IF YOU HAVE ANY. (PAUSE)

HE SAYS, "I HAVE GIVEN YOU THIS FAMILY SO THAT YOU MAY BE SURROUNDED WITH LOVE, THAT YOU LEARN RIGHT FROM WRONG, AND THAT YOU LEARN HOW TO SHARE YOUR LOVE WITH OTHERS. YOUR PARENTS WORK HARD TO PROVIDE YOU WITH FOOD, CLOTHING, AND SHELTER. THEY LOVE YOU, TEACH YOU THE FAITH, AND EDUCATE YOU. HOW CAN YOU MAKE A DIFFERENCE IN THEIR LIVES?"

YOU RESPOND, "I CAN SHOW MY LOVE FOR THEM BY OBEYING THEM BECAUSE, LIKE MY HEAVENLY FATHER, THEY KNOW WHAT IS BEST FOR ME. (PAUSE) I CAN DO MY CHORES WITH A SMILE ON MY FACE. I CAN BE SATISFIED WITH WHAT I HAVE AND NOT ASK FOR MORE. (PAUSE) I CAN ELIMINATE SOME OF THEIR WORRIES BY STAYING

OUT OF TROUBLE. I CAN GIVE THEM A HUG EACH NIGHT BEFORE I GO TO BED AND TELL THEM I LOVE THEM."

JESUS ANSWERS, "IF YOU DO ALL THESE THINGS YOU WILL BE PLEASING ME." HE THEN ASKS YOU, "HOW CAN YOU MAKE A DIFFERENCE IN THE LIVES OF YOUR BROTHERS AND SISTERS?"

YOU THINK FOR A MOMENT AND SAY, "I CAN BE THERE FOR THEM BY LISTENING TO THEM WHEN THEY NEED TO TALK, SHARING MY THINGS WITH THEM, HELPING THEM WHEN THEY NEED HELP, ENCOURAGING THEM WHEN THINGS ARE TOUGH, LAUGHING WITH THEM, PRAYING WITH THEM, AND GIVING THEM A HUG AND TELLING THEM I LOVE THEM." (PAUSE)

JESUS TELLS YOU, "YOUR FAMILY IS A SPECIAL GIFT I HAVE GIVEN YOU. PLEASE LOVE THEM AND CARE FOR THEM. DO ALL YOU CAN TO BRING HAPPINESS AND JOY TO THEM. THEY DESERVE IT."

YOU TURN TO JESUS AND SAY, "THANK YOU, DEAR JESUS, FOR THE WONDERFUL GIFT OF MY FAMILY AND FOR ALL THEY BRING TO MY LIFE. I WILL TREASURE THIS GIFT ALWAYS. (PAUSE)

"THANK YOU, DEAR JESUS, FOR OUR TIME TOGETHER TODAY. THANK YOU FOR BEING MY BIG BROTHER. PLEASE HELP ME MAKE A DIFFERENCE IN MY FAMILY EVERY DAY."

(SPEND A FEW MOMENTS IN SILENT PRAYER.)

DISCUSSION GUIDE

1. HOW CAN YOU MAKE A DIFFERENCE IN YOUR PARENTS' LIVES?

2. HOW CAN YOU MAKE A DIFFERENCE IN THE LIVES OF YOUR BROTHERS AND/OR SISTERS?

3. WHAT CAN YOU DO TO BRING HAPPINESS TO YOUR FAMILY?

4. DO YOU SPEND ENOUGH QUALITY TIME WITH YOUR FAMILY?

ADVENT: WEEK 1 - WAITING FOR CHRIST TO BE BORN IN OUR HEARTS

CLOSE YOUR EYES.

BREATHE IN, HOLD IT, BREATHE OUT. (3 TIMES)

YOU AND JESUS ARE STANDING ON A MOUNTAIN WAITING FOR THE SUN TO SET. (PAUSE) HE SAYS TO YOU, "HOW MANY TIMES HAVE YOU SAID, 'I CAN'T WAIT!'? THIS IS THE TIME OF YEAR YOU ARE WAITING TO CELEBRATE MY BIRTHDAY. YOU ARE WAITING FOR ME TO BE BORN IN YOUR HEART. (PAUSE) MY BIRTHDAY IS NOT ABOUT PRESENTS, BUT RATHER ABOUT THE GIFT OF MY PRESENCE, IN YOUR HEART. (PAUSE) MY PRESENCE WILL GIVE YOU JOY! A JOY THAT WILL LAST A LIFETIME." (PAUSE)

YOU LOOK AT JESUS AND SAY, "HOW DO I PREPARE FOR THIS GIFT OF YOUR PRESENCE IN MY HEART?"

JESUS ANSWERS, "PREPARE YOUR HEART TO BE THE PLACE OF MY BIRTH. CLEAN YOUR HEART OF SIN IN THE SACRAMENT OF RECONCILIATION, AND GROW IN VIRTUE. (PAUSE) LEARN TO GIVE MORE THAN YOU RECEIVE. BE SATISFIED WITH WHAT I HAVE GIVEN YOU INSTEAD OF WANTING MORE. (PAUSE) THE ONLY THING YOU SHOULD

WANT MORE OF IS ME IN YOUR LIFE. THEREIN LIES MY PRECIOUS GIFT OF JOY FOR YOU."

YOU ASK JESUS, "WHY DO YOU WANT TO COME INTO MY HEART?"

JESUS LOOKS AT YOU AND REPLIES, "I LOVE YOU, MY CHILD. I WAS BORN INTO THE WORLD TO SHOW YOU HOW TO LIVE YOUR LIFE TO THE FULLEST, TO BE ALL THAT YOU CAN BE FOR ME, AND TO MAKE A DIFFERENCE IN THE LIVES OF THOSE YOU MEET. (PAUSE) USE THE GIFTS AND TALENTS I HAVE GIVEN YOU TO PRAISE AND GLORIFY ME. (PAUSE) THIS IS THE BEST BIRTHDAY PRESENT YOU COULD GIVE ME."

YOU ASK JESUS, "PLEASE FILL ME WITH YOUR GRACE AND GIVE ME THE PATIENCE AND COURAGE TO LIVE MY LIFE IN THE WAY YOU WANT ME TO. HELP ME TO LET YOU BE REBORN IN THE HEARTS OF OTHERS THROUGH THE LOVE I SHOW THEM. (PAUSE) HELP ME TO BE YOU IN THE WORLD EACH DAY. THIS WILL BE MY GIFT TO YOU ON YOUR BIRTHDAY. THANK YOU FOR COMING INTO THE WORLD AND SHOWING US THE WAY TO LIVE OUR LIVES TO THE FULLEST AND, IN SO DOING, EXPERIENCE THE WONDERFUL GIFT OF YOUR JOY!"

TOGETHER YOU AND JESUS WATCH THE BEAUTIFUL RED AND ORANGE SUNSET. YOU WALK DOWN THE MOUNTAIN TOGETHER AND HE SAYS, "PEACE BE WITH YOU, MY CHILD," AND GIVES YOU A BIG HUG.

(SPEND A FEW MOMENTS IN SILENT PRAYER.)

DISCUSSION GUIDE

1. NAME SOME THINGS YOU CAN'T WAIT FOR.

2. WHAT IS IT THAT WE SHOULD WANT MORE THAN ANYTHING ELSE?

3. HOW CAN YOU MAKE A DIFFERENCE IN THE LIVES OF OTHERS?

4. NAME SOME GIFTS AND TALENTS GOD HAS GIVEN YOU.

5. HOW CAN YOU USE THESE GIFTS AND TALENTS TO SERVE GOD?

ADVENT: WEEK 2 - EMPTYING OUR HANDS TO HOLD JESUS

CLOSE YOUR EYES.

BREATHE IN, HOLD IT, BREATHE OUT. (3 TIMES)

YOU AND JESUS ARE SITTING ON THE BANK BY A STREAM. YOU CAN HEAR THE WATER TRICKLING OVER THE ROCKS. (PAUSE)

JESUS ASKS YOU TO HOLD OUT YOUR HANDS, PALMS UP. HE SAYS, "DURING THIS TIME OF ADVENT, I NEED YOU TO EMPTY YOUR HANDS OF THINGS LIKE SELFISHNESS AND GREED. NEVER TAKE MORE THAN YOU GIVE. THIS IS HOW YOU GET RID OF SELFISHNESS. (PAUSE) BE SATISFIED WITH WHAT YOU HAVE INSTEAD OF WANTING MORE. (PAUSE) THIS IS HOW YOU GET RID OF GREED. WHEN YOU EMPTY YOURSELF OF THESE THINGS, YOU WILL HAVE ROOM TO HOLD ME IN YOUR ARMS. THEN YOU CAN CARRY ME TO OTHERS." (PAUSE)

YOU ASK JESUS, "HOW CAN I CARRY YOU TO OTHERS?"

HE RESPONDS, "YOU CAN BRING ME TO OTHERS BY SPREADING MY JOY TO THEM. TELL THEM THAT YOU AND I LOVE THEM. GIVE THEM A HUG IF THEY NEED IT. (PAUSE) CRY WITH THEM AND CONSOLE THEM IF THEY NEED IT. (PAUSE) LAUGH WITH THEM IF THEY NEED TO

LAUGH. HELP THEM IF THEY NEED HELP. (PAUSE) PROMISE PRAYERS IF THEY ASK FOR THEM. (PAUSE) THESE ARE JUST A FEW WAYS TO BRING ME TO OTHERS. LET THAT BE YOUR CHRISTMAS GIFT TO THEM."

YOU LOOK AT JESUS AND SAY, "JESUS, I NEED YOUR HELP TO DO WHAT YOU ARE ASKING ME TO DO. PLEASE HELP ME TO BE GENEROUS INSTEAD OF SELFISH, TO BE SATISFIED WITH WHAT YOU HAVE SO GENEROUSLY GIVEN ME AND NOT WANT MORE. I WANT TO BRING YOU TO OTHERS EVERY DAY OF MY LIFE. (PAUSE) I WANT TO HOLD YOU IN MY ARMS ON CHRISTMAS DAY AND EVERY DAY OF THE YEAR. (PAUSE) I THANK YOU FOR THE SPECIAL GIFT OF YOU IN THE EUCHARIST. THIS IS YOUR BEST CHRISTMAS GIFT TO ALL OF US. (PAUSE) LET ME GROW IN MY LOVE FOR YOU EACH DAY."

YOU AND JEUS SIT QUIETLY TOGETHER, AND YOU PONDER ALL HE HAS SAID TO YOU.

YOU TURN TO JESUS AND SAY, "I AM GOING TO START EMPTYING MY HANDS TODAY SO I CAN FILL THEM WITH YOU AND THEN BRING YOU TO OTHERS. (PAUSE) THANK YOU FOR OUR TIME TOGETHER TODAY, AND I KNOW YOU WILL BE WITH ME ON THIS JOURNEY."

JESUS SAYS, "I CERTAINLY WILL -- NOW AND ALWAYS." HE THEN GIVES YOU A BIG HUG AND SAYS, "I LOVE YOU, MY CHILD."

YOU RESPOND, "I LOVE YOU TOO, JESUS."

(SPEND A FEW MOMENTS IN SILENT PRAYER.)

DISCUSSION GUIDE

1. WHAT DOES IT MEAN TO BE GREEDY?

2. WHAT DOES IT MEAN TO BE SELFISH?

3. HOW CAN YOU BE MORE GENEROUS WITH YOUR FAMILY?

4. HOW CAN YOU BE MORE GENEROUS WITH YOUR FRIENDS?

ADVENT: WEEK 3 - BE THE LIGHT OF CHRIST

CLOSE YOUR EYES.

BREATHE IN, HOLD IT, BREATHE OUT. (3 TIMES)

JESUS HAS TAKEN YOU TO A VERY DARK ROOM WHERE THERE ARE NO WINDOWS OR LIGHTS, JUST PITCH DARKNESS. (PAUSE)

HE SAYS TO YOU, "THIS IS WHAT THE WORLD WAS LIKE BEFORE I WAS BORN. PEOPLE WERE IN THE DARKNESS OF SIN. THEY WERE LONGING FOR MY COMING SO I WOULD TAKE AWAY THIS DARKNESS. (PAUSE) I WAS THE LIGHT THAT CAME INTO THE WORLD TO SHOW THEM THE WAY TO LIVE AND TO RID THEMSELVES OF THE DARKNESS OF SIN. (PAUSE) IT IS ONLY LIVING IN MY LIGHT THAT YOU CAN BRING LIGHT TO OTHERS."

YOU ASK, "DEAR JESUS, I WANT TO BE YOUR LIGHT IN THE WORLD. HOW CAN I DO THIS?

JESUS ANSWERS YOU BY SAYING, "FIRST, YOU MUST LEARN TO KNOW ME AND LOVE ME. SPEND TIME WITH ME EACH DAY, AND SEE HOW I WAS THE LIGHT IN THE WORLD. THEN IMITATE ME IN YOUR DAILY LIFE. (PAUSE) LIVING BY MY COMMANDMENTS IS MY LIGHT TO SHOW YOU THE WAY. BRINGING MY LIGHT TO OTHERS CAN

SHINE IN MANY WAYS . WHEN YOU OBEY YOUR PARENTS, YOU BRING THEM THE LIGHT OF MY PEACE. (PAUSE) WHEN YOU DO YOUR HOMEWORK NEATLY AND COMPLETELY, YOU BRING YOUR TEACHERS MY LIGHT OF HAPPINESS. (PAUSE) TREATING OTHERS WITH LOVE AND RESPECT WILL BRING THEM MY LIGHT OF JOY. (PAUSE) BEING GENTLE WITH YOUR BROTHERS AND SISTERS WILL BRING THEM MY LIGHT OF LOVE. (PAUSE) BE LIKE THE STAR OF BETHLEHEM THAT LIT UP THE NIGHT AND GUIDED THE SHEPHERDS AND THREE KINGS TO WITNESS MY HOLY BIRTH. YOU SERVE ME BEST WHEN YOU BRING THE LIGHT OF MY LOVE TO ALL THOSE YOU MEET EACH DAY."

YOU LOOK AT JESUS AND SAY, "I WILL BE YOUR LIGHT IN THE WORLD TODAY. OPEN MY EYES THAT I MIGHT RECOGNIZE WHEN I CAN BRING YOUR LIGHT TO OTHERS. MAKE ME AN INSTRUMENT OF YOUR LIGHT SHINING IN ME. (PAUSE) WHEN OTHERS SEE ME, LET THEM SEE YOU LIGHTING UP MY LIFE WITH YOUR PEACE, HAPPINESS, AND JOY. HELP ME BE THE NEW STAR OF BETHLEHEM THAT WILL LIGHT THE WAY AND BRING OTHERS TO YOU. THANK YOU, DEAR JESUS, FOR CALLING ME TO BE YOUR LIGHT IN THE WORLD TODAY."

BEFORE YOU AND JESUS LEAVE THE DARK ROOM, HE TURNS ON A LIGHT! YOU LOOK AT EACH OTHER WITH BIG SMILES ON YOUR FACE. HE PATS YOU ON THE BACK AND SAYS, "GO LIGHT UP THE WORLD!"

(SPEND A FEW MOMENTS IN SILENT PRAYER.)

DISCUSSION GUIDE

1. HOW DOES SIN BRING DARKNESS INTO YOUR LIFE?

2. NAME SOME WAYS YOU GET TO KNOW CHRIST.

    POSSIBLE ANSWERS:

    SCRIPTURE, PRAYER, THE CHURCH

3. IN WHAT WAYS CAN YOU IMITATE CHRIST?

4. NAME SOME WAYS YOU CAN LIGHT UP OTHERS' LIVES.

ADVENT: WEEK 4 - BE ANGELS OF THE LORD

CLOSE YOUR EYES.

BREATHE IN, HOLD IT, BREATHE OUT. (3 TIMES)

IT IS THE FIRST CHRISTMAS. YOU ARE AT THE STABLE IN BETHLEHEM WHERE JESUS IS LAYING IN THE MANGER. YOU ARE CELEBRATING HIS BIRTH WITH MARY AND JOSEPH. (PAUSE) HE INVITED YOU HERE TO REJOICE WITH THE ANGELS WHO ARE SINGING THEIR SONGS OF PRAISE. (PAUSE)

JESUS IS INVITING ALL OF US TO BE ANGELS HERE ON EARTH. YOU CAN BE HIS ANGEL OF MERCY BY FORGIVING OTHERS. (PAUSE) YOU CAN BE HIS ANGEL OF HOPE BY TELLING OTHERS TO TURN TO HIM IN THEIR TIMES OF SORROW AND DISAPPOINTMENT. (PAUSE) YOU CAN BE HIS ANGEL OF LOVE BY WHISPERING THE THREE WORDS "I LOVE YOU" TO OTHERS. (PAUSE) DON'T LET A DAY GO BY WITHOUT TELLING JESUS, YOUR FAMILY, AND FRIENDS THAT YOU LOVE THEM. (PAUSE) YOU CAN BE HIS ANGEL OF PEACE BY GETTING ALONG WITH OTHERS. YOU CAN BE HIS ANGEL OF GRATITUDE BY THANKING OTHERS FOR FORGIVING YOU, FOR GIVING YOU HOPE AND FOR GIVING YOU THEIR LOVE. (PAUSE) THESE PEOPLE ARE HIS ANGELS FOR YOU. (PAUSE)

BE THE ANGEL THAT TELLS THE GOOD NEWS OF HIS BIRTH AND ABOUT HIS LIFE HERE ON EARTH. WATCH HIM BEING BORN IN ALL THOSE YOU MEET, AND GREET HIM WITH GLAD TIDINGS OF JOY! (PAUSE)

JESUS IS BEING REBORN IN YOU EVERY SECOND OF EVERY DAY WHEN YOU ARE BEING HIS ANGEL. LET YOUR LIFE AND YOUR LOVE BE A SONG TO PRAISE GOD. (PAUSE) LET YOUR ARMS BE YOUR ANGEL WINGS WHICH EMBRACE ALL THOSE YOU MEET. LET YOUR ANGEL EYES LOOK AT OTHERS AND FIND CHRIST IN THEM. (PAUSE) LET YOUR ANGEL FEET WALK IN THE PATH THAT CHRIST HAS MAPPED OUT FOR YOU. LET YOUR ANGEL HAND HOLD ONTO CHRIST'S HAND THROUGHOUT YOUR JOURNEY. (PAUSE)

LET US CELEBRATE HIS BIRTHDAY WITH JOY IN OUR HEARTS. (PAUSE) LET US THANK HIM FOR COMING TO EARTH AND SHOWING US THE WAY TO LIVE. (PAUSE) LET'S SING OUR HEARTS OUT AT CHRISTMAS MASS AND RECEIVE HIM IN OUR HEART. (PAUSE) LET HIM LIVE THERE EACH DAY OF THE YEAR SO THAT EACH DAY IS CHRISTMAS! (PAUSE)

(SPEND A FEW MOMENTS IN SILENT PRAYER.)

DISCUSSION GUIDE

1. HOW DOES FORGIVING OTHERS HELP YOUR RELATIONSHIP WITH THEM?

2. NAME SOME WAYS YOU CAN FIND CHRIST IN OTHERS.

3. WHAT ARE SOME OF THE PRESENTS CHRIST GIVES YOU?

4. WHAT IS THE BEST GIFT YOU CAN GIVE TO JESUS ON HIS BIRTHDAY?

JANUARY: WEEK 1 - SNOWFLAKES

CLOSE YOUR EYES.

BREATHE IN, HOLD IT, BREATHE OUT. (3 TIMES)

YOU AND JESUS ARE STANDING ON A SNOW-COVERED HILL, BUNDLED IN YOUR WINTER CLOTHING, WAITING TO SLIDE DOWN THE HILL ON A TOBOGGAN. YOU ARE BOTH WATCHING SNOWFLAKES QUIETLY FALLING. (PAUSE)

JESUS SAYS, "YOU KNOW ALL HUMAN BEINGS ARE LIKE SNOWFLAKES. THERE ARE NO TWO ALIKE. EACH ONE IS DIFFERENT FROM THE OTHER. (PAUSE) IN ALL OF CREATION THERE IS NO OTHER HUMAN BEING LIKE YOU. YOU ARE UNIQUE AND SPECIAL TO ME. (PAUSE) I HAVE CREATED YOU TO BE ME IN THE WORLD. YOUR EYES ARE MY EYES. USE THEM TO LOOK FOR ME IN OTHERS. (PAUSE) YOUR HANDS ARE MY HANDS. USE THEM TO SERVE ME BY SERVING OTHERS. (PAUSE) YOUR FEET ARE MY FEET. USE THEM TO WALK THE PATH I HAVE PLANNED FOR YOU. (PAUSE) YOUR MOUTH IS MY MOUTH. USE IT TO SPEAK MY WORDS OF LOVE TO OTHERS. YOUR EARS ARE MY EARS. USE THEM TO LISTEN TO THE GOOD NEWS I HAVE PROCLAIMED TO THE WORLD, TO LISTEN TO OTHERS MORE, AND TO SPEAK LESS. (PAUSE) LET ME LIVE THROUGH YOU!"

YOU RESPOND, "JESUS, I WANT TO BE YOU IN THE WORLD. I DEDICATE THE REST OF MY LIFE TO YOU TODAY. I WILL BE YOUR EYES THAT OTHERS MAY SEE YOUR LOOK OF COMPASSION AND LOVE IN THEM. (PAUSE) I WILL BE YOUR HANDS THAT THROUGH MY SERVICE TO OTHERS YOU WILL LET THEM KNOW YOU LOVE THEM SO MUCH. (PAUSE) I WILL BE YOUR FEET TO WALK IN YOUR PATH WHEREVER YOU MAY LEAD ME. (PAUSE) I WILL BE YOUR MOUTH TO SAY TO OTHERS THE THREE WORDS, 'I LOVE YOU' THEY WANT TO HEAR. (PAUSE) I WILL BE YOUR EARS TO LISTEN TO YOUR WORDS OF KNOWLEDGE AND WISDOM AND TO LISTEN TO OTHERS MORE. (PAUSE) I THANK YOU FOR THE GIFT OF MY LIFE, AND I ASK THAT YOU PLEASE GIVE ME THE GRACE AND COURAGE TO CARRY OUT YOUR WORK HERE ON EARTH." (PAUSE)

JESUS LOOKS INTO YOUR EYES AND SAYS, "THANK YOU, MY CHILD, AND I DO CONTINUALLY GIVE YOU THE GRACE TO BE ME IN THE WORLD. ALL YOU HAVE TO DO IS ACCEPT IT." (PAUSE)

YOU AND JESUS GET ON THE TOBOGGAN AND FLY DOWN THE HILL TOGETHER. WHAT A GLORIOUS AND FUN RIDE! HE GIVES YOU A HIGH-FIVE AND SAYS, "LET YOUR LIFE BE AS GLORIOUS AND FUN AS THAT RIDE WAS AND KNOW THAT I LOVE YOU VERY MUCH."

(SPEND A FEW MOMENTS IN SILENT PRAYER.)

DISCUSSION GUIDE

1. HOW CAN YOU USE YOUR EYES TO BECOME ALL GOD WANTS YOU TO BE?

2. HOW CAN YOU USE YOUR HANDS TO BECOME ALL GOD WANTS YOU TO BE?

3. HOW CAN YOU USE YOUR FEET TO BECOME ALL GOD WANTS YOU TO BE?

4. HOW CAN YOU USE YOUR MOUTH TO BECOME ALL GOD WANTS YOU TO BE?

JANUARY: WEEK 2 - THE SEED OF FAITH NEEDS PRAYER

CLOSE YOUR EYES..

BREATHE IN, HOLD IT, BREATHE OUT. (3 TIMES)

YOU AND JESUS ARE IN A GREENHOUSE LOOKING AT THE BEAUTY OF ALL THE PLANTS AND FLOWERS. (PAUSE)

JESUS SAYS TO YOU, "ALL THESE PLANTS BEGAN TO GROW FROM JUST A TINY SEED. THEY NEED WATER AND SUNLIGHT TO GROW. (PAUSE) I HAVE PLANTED THE SEED OF FAITH IN YOU SO THAT YOUR SOUL MAY GROW AND BLOSSOM INTO THE FLOWER I MEANT YOU TO BE. (PAUSE) I HAVE WATERED YOUR SOUL WITH THE SACRAMENT OF BAPTISM, WHICH IS EVERLASTING WATER. I AM THE ETERNAL LIGHT THAT SHINES UPON YOU EACH DAY. (PAUSE) BESIDES WATER AND LIGHT, YOUR SPIRITUAL LIFE NEEDS PRAYER. PRAYER IS THE FERTILIZER FOR YOUR SOUL. (PAUSE) BEGIN YOUR DAY BY ADORING, PRAISING, AND LOVING ME. SAY A PRAYER OF THANKSGIVING FOR YOUR LIFE AND FOR MY CONTINUOUS BLESSINGS UPON YOU. (PAUSE) CONTINUE YOUR PRAYER THROUGHOUT THE DAY BY LOOKING FOR AND FINDING ME IN OTHERS. OFFER ME YOUR LOVE IN EVERYTHING THAT YOU DO. (PAUSE) END EACH DAY WITH EVENING PRAYER. (PAUSE)

"MANY PEOPLE SAY THAT THEY DON'T HAVE TIME TO PRAY. HOW SAD! THEY FIND TIME FOR TV, COMPUTER GAMES, TEXTING, ETC. (PAUSE) SO PRAY, MY DEAR CHILD, EVERY DAY SO THAT WHEN YOU ENTER ETERNITY, YOU WILL BE THE FLOWER IN MY HEAVENLY GARDEN."

YOU LOOK AT JESUS AND SAY, "DEAR JESUS, I WILL PUT PRAYER FIRST IN MY LIFE. I WILL GET UP TEN MINUTES EARLIER TO SAY MY MORNING PRAYERS. I WILL GO TO BED TEN MINUTES EARLIER TO SAY MY EVENING PRAYERS. THROUGHOUT THE DAY, I WILL LOOK FOR YOU IN OTHERS AND SERVE YOU. (PAUSE) HELP ME, DEAR JESUS, TO KEEP MY PROMISE TO YOU TO PRAY EACH DAY. MY LIFE BEGAN WITH YOU, AND I WANT IT TO END WITH ME BEING A BEAUTIFUL FLOWER IN YOUR HEAVENLY GARDEN."

JESUS REPLIES, "I LOOK FORWARD TO HEARING FROM YOU EACH DAY BECAUSE I KNOW THROUGH DAILY PRAYER YOU WILL COME CLOSER TO ME. NOW, GO IN PEACE, MY CHILD, AND LIVE YOUR JOYOUS FAITH."

(SPEND A FEW MOMENTS IN SILENT PRAYER.)

DISCUSSION GUIDE

1. HOW MANY HOURS A DAY DO YOU THINK YOU SPEND EITHER PLAYING VIDEO GAMES, WATCHING T.V., ON THE COMPUTER, OR TEXTING?

2. LET'S ADD UP ALL THOSE HOURS AND SEE HOW MANY HOURS PER DAY YOU SPEND DOING WHAT YOU <u>THINK</u> IS SO IMPORTANT.

3. THIS IS THE TOTAL: _____. HOW MANY OF YOU THINK THAT YOU COULD SPEND AT LEAST TEN MINUTES PER DAY <u>PRAYING</u> INSTEAD OF DOING THESE OTHERS THINGS?

4. HOW COULD YOU SCHEDULE PRAYER IN YOUR DAY?

<u>POSSIBLE ANSWERS:</u>

--get up ten minutes earlier

--go to bed ten minutes earlier

--while riding in the car

--during quiet times throughout the day

JANUARY: WEEK 3 - BEING RELIABLE

CLOSE YOUR EYES.

BREATHE IN, HOLD IT, BREATHE OUT. (3 TIMES)

YOU AND JESUS ARE SITTING ON A BOULDER HIGH ABOVE THE OCEAN ENJOYING A REFRESHING BREEZE AND THE KISS OF THE SUN. (PAUSE)

JESUS SAYS THAT HE WANTS TO TALK TO YOU TODAY ABOUT THE MEANING OF THE WORD *RELIABLE*. HE SAYS, "LET'S BREAK THE WORD INTO TWO PARTS. *LIABLE* MEANS TO BE RESPONSIBLE. THE PREFIX *re* MEANS OVER AND OVER AGAIN. SO THE WORD *RELIABLE* MEANS TO BE RESPONSIBLE OVER AND OVER AGAIN. (PAUSE) MY HEAVENLY FATHER COULD RELY ON ME TO COMMUNICATE WITH HIM EVERY DAY IN PRAYER. HE COULD RELY ON ME TO CARRY OUT HIS WILL EVERY DAY OF MY LIFE. (PAUSE) PEOPLE COULD RELY ON ME TO BE THERE FOR THEM WHETHER IT WAS THROUGH MY TEACHING THEM THE TRUTH, LISTENING TO THEM, OR HEALING THEM. THEY KNEW I CARED ABOUT THEM EVEN TO THE POINT OF GIVING UP MY LIFE FOR THEM! (PAUSE)

"MY FATHER RELIES ON YOU EACH DAY TO CARRY OUT THE MISSION HE HAS PLANNED FOR YOU. TO CARRY OUT HIS MISSION YOU MUST EMBRACE THE FACT THAT PEOPLE

RELY ON YOU TO HELP THEM CARRY OUT THEIR MISSION, TOO. (PAUSE) YOUR PARENTS RELY ON YOU TO DO YOUR PART IN THE FAMILY. YOUR FRIENDS RELY ON YOU TO BE THERE FOR THEM. (PAUSE) TEACHERS RELY ON YOU TO TURN YOUR WORK IN ON TIME AND TO STUDY FOR TESTS. SO BE RESPONSIBLE OVER AND OVER AGAIN."

YOU RESPOND, "DEAR JESUS, I KNOW I CAN IMPROVE IN THIS AREA, AND I DO WANT TO BE A MORE RELIABLE PERSON. I ASK FOR YOUR HELP, AND I PROMISE I WILL WORK ON IT MORE AND MORE EACH DAY. I WANT SO MUCH TO BE LIKE YOU."

JESUS LOOKS YOU IN THE EYE AND SAYS, "I AM COUNTING ON YOU TO DO YOUR BEST, AND I WILL HELP YOU. YOU KNOW YOU CAN RELY ON ME TO ALWAYS BE THERE FOR YOU. NOW GO IN PEACE, MY CHILD."

YOU SAY, "THANK YOU, DEAR JESUS, FOR ANOTHER VALUABLE LESSON. I LOOK FORWARD TO YOUR NEXT LESSON IN HELPING ME LIVE MY LIFE TO THE FULLEST."

(SPEND A FEW MOMENTS IN SILENT PRAYER.)

DISCUSSION GUIDE

1. HOW DO YOUR PARENTS RELY ON YOU?

2. HOW DO YOUR FRIENDS RELY ON YOU?

3. HOW DO YOUR TEACHERS RELY ON YOU?

4. IN WHAT AREAS CAN YOU BE MORE RELIABLE?

JANUARY: WEEK 4 - RESPONSIBILITY TO YOURSELF

CLOSE YOUR EYES.

BREATHE IN, HOLD IT, BREATHE OUT. (3 TIMES)

YOUR PHONE RINGS. YOU PICK IT UP AND SAY, "HELLO. MAY I ASK WHO IS CALLING?"

THE VOICE ON THE OTHER END SAYS, "THIS IS YOUR BEST FRIEND, JESUS. DO YOU HAVE TIME TO TALK TO ME?"

YOU ANSWER, "OF COURSE, JESUS. WHAT WOULD YOU LIKE TO TALK TO ME ABOUT?" (PAUSE)

JESUS SAYS, "I WOULD LIKE TO TALK TO YOU ABOUT THE RESPONSIBILITY YOU HAVE TO YOURSELF. I AM ASKING YOU TO BE RESPONSIBLE FOR YOUR SPIRITUAL, PHYSICAL, EMOTIONAL, AND INTELLECTUAL WELL-BEING. YOUR SPIRITUAL LIFE MUST GROW THROUGH PRAYER. (PAUSE) YOUR PHYSICAL LIFE NEEDS HEALTHY FOODS, SUFFICIENT REST, AND EXERCISE. (PAUSE) YOUR EMOTIONAL LIFE NEEDS LOVE -- THE LOVE YOU GET FROM OTHERS AND YOUR LOVE FOR OTHERS. (PAUSE) YOUR INTELLECTUAL LIFE NEEDS KNOWLEDGE TO GROW. THESE ARE ALL IMPORTANT TO LIVE A FULL AND MEANINGFUL LIFE. ARE YOU TAKING CARE OF THESE AREAS?"

"WELL, DEAR JESUS, I COULD BE MORE RESPONSIBLE IN THESE AREAS, ESPECIALLY IN MY SPIRITUAL LIFE. I LONG FOR A DEEPER RELATIONSHIP WITH YOU AND I KNOW I CAN DO THAT THROUGH PRAYER. I PROMISE I WILL TRY TO DO THAT MORE OFTEN."

JESUS REPLIES, "GOOD START, MY CHILD. WHAT ABOUT YOUR PHYSICAL LIFE? WHAT CAN YOU DO TO MAKE THAT BETTER?"

YOU ANSWER, "WELL, DEAR JESUS, I COULD GIVE UP THE JUNK FOOD I EAT, GET MORE EXERCISE, AND GET A GOOD NIGHT'S SLEEP. I KNOW MY BODY NEEDS THESE THINGS, AND I WANT TO STAY HEALTHY SO I CAN CARRY OUT THE MISSION YOU HAVE GIVEN ME IN MY LIFE."

JESUS SAYS, "YES, THAT IS VERY IMPORTANT TO TAKE CARE OF YOUR PHYSICAL WELL-BEING. HOW ARE THINGS FOR YOU EMOTIONALLY? "

YOU RESPOND, "WELL, DEAR JESUS, I KNOW MY FAMILY AND FRIENDS LOVE ME, AND I THANK YOU FOR THEM. I AM TRYING TO LOVE OTHERS MORE BY SEEING YOU IN THEM. I AM LEARNING TO LAUGH, CRY, AND HAVE FUN WITH YOU THROUGH THEM. I PROMISE I WILL TRY TO SEE YOU IN OTHERS MORE."

JESUS SAYS, "YOU ARE ON THE RIGHT TRACK. KEEP SEARCHING FOR ME IN OTHERS. YOU WILL MEET ME IN OTHERS MANY TIMES EACH DAY. NOW, HOW IS YOUR INTELLECTUAL LIFE GROWING?"

YOU ANSWER, "DEAR LORD, I AM LEARNING MANY NEW THINGS IN SCHOOL EACH DAY. YOU HAVE GIVEN ME GENEROUS PARENTS WHO WANT THE BEST EDUCATION FOR ME, WONDERFUL TEACHERS WHO CARE ABOUT ME, AND GREAT CLASSMATES WITH WHOM I CAN SHARE

MY SCHOOL YEARS. I PROMISE I WILL DO MY BEST IN MY STUDIES AND USE THE BRAINS YOU'VE GIVEN ME SO I CAN SERVE YOU BY SERVING YOUR PEOPLE IN THE WORLD. THANK YOU FOR POINTING OUT THESE AREAS FOR ME TO WORK ON. I WANT TO BE THE BEST CHRISTIAN I CAN BE."

JESUS SAYS, "I PROMISE, MY CHILD, I AM WITH YOU ON YOUR JOURNEY. I AM COUNTING ON YOU. HAVE A WONDERFUL DAY AND KNOW THAT I AM ALWAYS WITH YOU AND LOVING YOU."

YOU END YOUR CONVERSATION WITH JESUS SAYING, "I LOVE YOU, TOO, DEAR LORD. I LOOK FORWARD TO HEARING FROM YOU AGAIN."

(SPEND A FEW MOMENTS IN SILENT PRAYER.)

DISCUSSION GUIDE

1. HOW CAN YOU IMPROVE SPIRITUALLY?

2. HOW CAN YOU IMPROVE PHYSICALLY?

3. HOW CAN YOU IMPROVE EMOTIONALLY?

4. HOW CAN YOU IMPROVE INTELLECTUALLY?

FEBRUARY: WEEK 1 - RESPONSIBILITY TO OTHERS

CLOSE YOUR EYES.

BREATHE IN, HOLD IT, BREATHE OUT. (3 TIMES)

YOU AND JESUS ARE TAKING A LEISURELY WALK IN YOUR NEIGHBORHOOD. HE BEGINS TALKING TO YOU ABOUT THE RESPONSIBILITY WE ALL HAVE TO OTHERS.

HE ASKS, "DID YOU KNOW THAT YOU HAVE A RESPONSIBILITY TO ME, YOUR FAMILY AND FRIENDS, THE EARTH, AND ANIMALS?"

YOU ASK HIM TO PLEASE TELL YOU WHAT THESE RESPONSIBILITIES ARE.

HE BEGINS BY SAYING, "YOUR RESPONSIBILITY TO ME IS TO BE ALL THAT I HAVE CREATED YOU TO BE SO THAT YOU CAN SERVE ME IN YOUR LIFETIME. (PAUSE) I LONG TO HEAR FROM YOU EACH DAY. ASK ME FOR HELP LIVING YOUR LIFE. TELL ME YOUR CONCERNS. TELL ME YOUR DREAMS. (PAUSE) TRUST IN ME ALWAYS. I WILL GUIDE YOU IN BECOMING THE PERSON I INTENDED YOU TO BE. DO YOU BELIEVE THAT?"

YOU ANSWER, "YES, DEAR JESUS, I DO. HOWEVER, I NEED YOUR HELP IN LEARNING TO TRUST YOU MORE AND TO

BELIEVE THAT YOU KNOW WHAT IS BEST FOR ME. PLEASE HELP ME ON THIS."

JESUS LOOKS AT YOU LOVINGLY AND SAYS, "I ALWAYS KNOW WHAT IS BEST FOR YOU. I ASK THAT YOU ONLY TRUST ME. (PAUSE) I WANT YOU TO KNOW THAT YOU HAVE A RESPONSIBILITY TO YOUR FAMILY AND FRIENDS ALSO. YOUR FAMILY NEEDS YOU TO BE A LOVING, CARING, THOUGHTFUL, AND RESPONSIBLE PERSON SO YOU CAN ALL LIVE IN HARMONY. (PAUSE) YOUR FRIENDS NEED TO COUNT ON YOU TO BE THERE FOR THEM, WHETHER IT IS HAVING FUN TOGETHER, SHARING SECRETS, SUCCESSES, SORROWS, OR SADNESS. (PAUSE) SOMETIMES YOU ARE THE ONLY ONE TO WHOM THEY CAN TURN. MAKE TIME FOR THEM."

YOU RESPOND, "DEAR JESUS, YOU ARE SO RIGHT! I LOVE THE FAMILY AND ALL THE DEAR FRIENDS YOU HAVE GIVEN ME. I AM VERY BLESSED, AND I THANK YOU. I PROMISE I WILL DO MY BEST TO SHOW THEM MY LOVE."

JESUS CONTINUES BY SAYING, "YOU KNOW YOU ALSO HAVE A RESPONSIBILITY TO CARE FOR THE EARTH AND ALL THE ANIMALS THAT SHARE IT WITH YOU. TREAT THEM BOTH WITH LOVE AND RESPECT AND CARE FOR THEM SO THAT FUTURE GENERATIONS CAN ENJOY THEM, TOO." (PAUSE)

YOU RESPOND, "I WILL, DEAR JESUS, AND I THANK YOU FOR YOUR BEAUTIFUL EARTH AND ALL THE WONDERFUL ANIMALS. I PROMISE I WILL DO MY PART IN CARING FOR THEM."

YOU AND JESUS HAVE FINISHED YOUR WALK TOGETHER AND JESUS SAYS, "THANK YOU, MY DEAR FRIEND, FOR LISTENING TO ME, AND I COUNT ON YOU TO KEEP YOUR PROMISES."

YOU ANSWER, " YOU CAN COUNT ON ME, JESUS. I ENJOYED OUR WALK AND TALK TODAY AND LOOK FORWARD TO HEARING FROM YOU AGAIN."

JESUS SAYS, "OH, YOU CAN COUNT ON THAT!"

(SPEND A FEW MOMENTS IN SILENT PRAYER.)

DISCUSSION GUIDE

1. HOW CAN YOU BECOME ALL THAT GOD WANTS YOU TO BE?

   POSSIBLE ANSWERS:

   ---prayer

   ---developing your talents and gifts

   ---doing your best in school

2. HOW CAN YOU BECOME A BETTER MEMBER OF YOUR FAMILY?

3. HOW CAN YOU BE MORE RESPONSIBLE IN YOUR FRIENDSHIPS?

4. IN WHAT WAYS CAN YOU CARE FOR THE EARTH?

5. IN WHAT WAYS CAN YOU CARE FOR ANIMALS?

FEBRUARY: WEEK 2 - UNCONDITIONAL LOVE - (FOR VALENTINE'S DAY)

CLOSE YOUR EYES.

BREATHE IN, HOLD IT, BREATHE OUT. (3 TIMES)

YOU HEAR YOUR DOORBELL RING. WHEN YOU OPEN THE DOOR, JESUS IS STANDING THERE WITH A BIG SMILE ON HIS FACE WAITING FOR YOU TO INVITE HIM IN. WHEN YOU INVITE HIM IN, HE GIVES YOU A BIG HUG AND SAYS,"I AM SO GLAD TO SEE YOU. DO YOU HAVE TIME FOR A LITTLE CHIT CHAT WITH ME?"

YOU SAY, "OF COURSE, JESUS. YOU ARE MY BEST FRIEND. COME AND SIT WITH ME."

JESUS ASKS, "DO YOU KNOW WHAT UNCONDITIONAL LOVE IS?"

YOU ANSWER, "I'M NOT SURE, JESUS. COULD YOU PLEASE EXPLAIN IT TO ME?"

JESUS SAYS, "IT MEANS, UNDER NO CONDITION, WILL I EVER STOP LOVING YOU. NO MATTER WHAT YOU SAY OR DO, I WILL ALWAYS LOVE YOU. (PAUSE) I HAVE GIVEN YOU A FREE WILL. YOU CAN <u>CHOOSE</u> TO HAVE ME IN

YOUR LIFE OR NOT, BUT I WILL NEVER STOP LOVING YOU. (PAUSE) I AM CHASING YOU EVERY MOMENT OF EVERY DAY AND WILL PATIENTLY WAIT FOR YOU TO TURN AROUND, EMBRACE ME, AND FOLLOW ME. (PAUSE) IT IS YOUR CHOICE! IF YOU CHOOSE TO FOLLOW ME I CAN PROMISE YOU A LIFE OF TREMENDOUS PEACE, HAPPINESS, AND JOY. ISN'T THAT WHAT YOU REALLY WANT IN YOUR LIFE, MY CHILD?"

YOU SAY, "YOU BET, DEAR JESUS." YOU GET UP AND WALK OVER TO JESUS AND SAY, "YOU CAN STOP CHASING ME NOW." YOU EMBRACE HIM AND SAY, " I WANT TO FOLLOW YOU AND BE MORE LIKE YOU IN ALL I SAY AND DO. I WANT TO LET OTHERS KNOW I LOVE THEM, TOO."

WHILE THE TWO OF YOU EMBRACE ONE ANOTHER WITH BIG SMILES ON YOUR FACES, JESUS SAYS, "YOU KNOW, YOU HAVE A PERFECT OPPORTUNITY THIS WEEK, ON VALENTINE'S DAY, TO DO JUST THAT. WHEN YOU ARE MAKING OUT YOUR VALENTINE'S DAY CARDS, I ENCOURAGE YOU TO WRITE AT LEAST ONE THING YOU LIKE ABOUT THE PERSON TO WHOM YOU ARE GIVING IT. YOU MIGHT BE SURPRISED AT HOW THAT WILL MAKE A BIG DIFFERENCE TO THEM. THAT IS LOVE IN ACTION!"

YOU RESPOND, "YOU KNOW, DEAR JESUS, THAT IS A GREAT IDEA, AND I'M GOING TO DO THAT. THAT WILL BE MY VALENTINE TO YOU."

JESUS LOOKS AT YOU AND SAYS, "AND MY VALENTINE TO YOU IS THAT I WILL ALWAYS LOVE YOU NO MATTER WHAT. DON'T EVER FORGET THAT."

(SPEND A FEW MOMENTS IN SILENT PRAYER.)

DISCUSSION GUIDE

1. WHAT DOES GIVING VALENTINE'S DAY CARDS MEAN TO YOU?

2. HOW MANY OF YOU ARE WILLING TO WRITE ONE GOOD THING ABOUT THE PERSON TO WHOM YOU ARE GIVING IT?

3. DO YOU THINK YOUR MESSAGE TO THEM WILL MAKE A DIFFERENCE?

4. IN WHAT WAYS TO YOU THINK IT WILL MAKE A DIFFERENCE?

LENT: ASH WEDNESDAY

CLOSE YOUR EYES.

BREATHE IN, HOLD IT, BREATHE OUT. (3 TIMES)

YOU AND JESUS ARE WATCHING A FIRE BURN UNTIL THERE IS NOTHING LEFT BUT A PILE OF ASHES. (PAUSE)

HE SAYS, "ASH WEDNESDAY IS THE BEGINNING OF A FORTY DAY PREPARATION TO CELEBRATE MY PASSION, DEATH, AND THEN MY RESURRECTION ON EASTER SUNDAY. ASHES ARE A SYMBOL OF OUR DEATH TO SIN, WHICH IS WHAT WE ARE CALLED TO DO DURING LENT. I WOULD LIKE TO HELP YOU DURING THIS TIME OF PREPARATION. WOULD YOU LIKE TO DO THAT WITH ME?"

YOU ANSWER, "YES, DEAR LORD. I AM READY TO LISTEN TO YOU."

JESUS SAYS, "I ENCOURAGE YOU TO GROW IN YOUR LOVE FOR ME BY WORKING ON A SPECIFIC VIRTUE THAT WILL HELP YOU BECOME MORE LIKE ME. A VIRTUE IS SOMETHING THAT SHOWS YOU ARE A GOOD PERSON. HONESTY, FIDELITY, AND PATIENCE ARE JUST A FEW. (PAUSE) THINK OF ONE THAT YOU COULD WORK ON EACH DAY THAT WOULD HELP YOU GROW TO BE MORE LIKE ME. (PAUSE) IF YOU HAVE A HARD TIME TELLING THE TRUTH, THEN WORK ON BEING HONEST. IF YOU HAVE A HARD TIME BEING FAITHFUL TO ME AND MY TEACHINGS OR

BEING FAITHFUL TO YOUR FAMILY AND FRIENDS, THEN WORK ON BEING MORE FAITHFUL. IF YOU HAVE A HARD TIME BEING PATIENT, THEN PRACTICE THAT VIRTUE. DO YOU UNDERSTAND WHAT I MEAN?"

YOU RESPOND, "YES, DEAR LORD, AND I DO HAVE ONE I CAN WORK ON EACH DAY. WHATEVER HELPS ME BECOME MORE LIKE YOU IS WHAT I WILL DO."

JESUS GOES ON TO SAY, "LENT IS ALSO A TIME TO DO PENANCE, WHICH IS ANOTHER VIRTUE. DOING PENANCE IS A WAY OF EXPRESSING SORROW FOR OUR SINS, AND IT HELPS US TO AVOID FUTURE SIN. SELF-DENIAL IS A GOOD WAY OF DOING PENANCE. FOR EXAMPLE, DENY YOURSELF OF EATING MORE THAN YOU REALLY NEED. DENY YOURSELF OF WATCHING TOO MUCH TV, OR SPENDING HOURS ON THE COMPUTER OR TEXTING. RATHER USE THIS TECHNOLOGY FOR DOING GOOD. (PAUSE) THINK OF ONE THING OF WHICH YOU CAN DENY YOURSELF. DO THIS DURING LENT, AND IF YOU ARE FAITHFUL IN DOING IT, IT WILL BECOME A NEW AND BETTER HABIT. SELF-DENIAL WILL HELP YOU GROW SPIRITUALLY."

YOU TURN TO JESUS AND SAY, "THANK YOU, DEAR LORD, FOR YOUR DIRECTION IN MY SPIRITUAL LIFE. I WILL SPEND THESE FORTY DAYS WORKING ON GROWING IN VIRTUE AND PRACTICING SELF-DENIAL. MAY I HAVE YOUR BLESSING AND GRACE TO DO THIS?"

JESUS BLESSES YOU AND PROMISES HIS GRACE FOR YOU. HE SAYS, "TRUST IN ME TO BE WITH YOU ON YOUR LENTEN JOURNEY."

(SPEND A FEW MOMENTS IN SILENT PRAYER.)

DISCUSSION GUIDE

1. WHAT ARE SOME VIRTUES YOU COULD WORK ON DURING LENT?

2. HOW DOES DOING PENANCE HELP US BECOME BETTER CHRISTIANS?

3. GIVE SOME SUGGESTIONS OF HOW YOU COULD PRACTICE SELF-DENIAL.

4. WHY IS SELF-DENIAL BENEFICIAL?

SUGGESTED ACTIVITY

HAVE STUDENTS WRITE DOWN ONE VIRTUE THEY ARE GOING TO PRACTICE AND ONE AREA IN WHICH THEY ARE GOING TO PRACTICE SELF-DENIAL. TELL STUDENTS TO CHECK THIS LIST EACH NIGHT TO SEE IF THEY DID WHAT THEY SAID THEY WERE GOING TO DO.

LENT: AGONY IN THE GARDEN

CLOSE YOUR EYES.

BREATHE IN, HOLD IT, BREATHE OUT. (3 TIMES)

JESUS HAS ASKED YOU TO TAKE A WALK WITH HIM INTO THE GARDEN OF GETHSEMANE. HE SAYS, "I WANT TO TELL YOU ABOUT THE NIGHT I PRAYED HERE BEFORE I WAS ARRESTED. I INVITED PETER, JAMES, AND JOHN TO PRAY WITH ME. I WAS IN GREAT AGONY KNOWING WHAT MY FATHER WANTED OF ME. I FELL ON THE GROUND AND PRAYED, "ABBA, FATHER, EVERYTHING IS POSSIBLE TO YOU. TAKE THIS CUP FROM ME --BUT NOT WHAT I WILL, BUT WHAT YOU WILL." I WENT BACK AND FOUND MY APOSTLES SLEEPING. I SAID TO PETER, "SIMON, ARE YOU ASLEEP? COULD YOU NOT KEEP WATCH FOR ONE HOUR? WATCH AND PRAY THAT YOU MAY NOT UNDERGO THE TEST. THE SPIRIT IS WILLING BUT THE FLESH IS WEAK." I WENT BACK AGAIN AND PRAYED TO MY FATHER SAYING THE SAME THING. I RETURNED ONCE MORE AND FOUND THEM ASLEEP, FOR THEY COULD NOT KEEP THEIR EYES OPEN, AND THEY DID NOT KNOW WHAT TO SAY TO ME. I RETURNED A THIRD TIME AND SAID TO THEM, "ARE YOU STILL SLEEPING AND TAKING YOUR REST? IT IS ENOUGH. THE HOUR HAS COME. BEHOLD, THE SON OF MAN IS TO BE HANDED OVER TO SINNERS. GET UP. LET US GO. SEE, MY BETRAYER IS AT HAND" (BASED ON THE GOSPEL OF MATTHEW 14:32-42).

"WILLIAM BARCLAY, THE AUTHOR OF THE DAILY STUDY BIBLE SERIES, EXPLAINS THAT THERE WERE TWO THINGS I WANTED THAT NIGHT. ONE WAS TO HAVE THE COMPANIONSHIP OF MY FOLLOWERS, AND THE OTHER ONE WAS THAT I WANTED MY FATHER TO TAKE HIS CROSS FROM ME. I GOT NEITHER. (PAUSE) INSTEAD, I ACCEPTED ALL THAT MY FATHER HAD PLANNED FOR ME. I KNEW I WAS GOING TO BE CRUCIFIED AND I KNEW THE HORROR OF THAT KIND OF DEATH. I DID NOT WANT TO DIE. I WAS ONLY THIRTY-THREE YEARS OLD AND COULD HAVE DONE SO MUCH MORE GOOD. I DID NOT FULLY UNDERSTAND WHY IT HAD TO BE THE WAY MY FATHER WANTED IT. HOWEVER, I CARRIED OUT MY FATHER'S WILL, WITHOUT ANY DOUBT. I COULD HAVE RUN AWAY WHEN THEY CAME TO ARREST ME, BUT IF I HAD, I WOULD HAVE BETRAYED MY FATHER. I FACED WHAT THE FATHER WANTED ME TO DO, AND I WAS FAITHFUL TILL THE END. I SAVED THE WHOLE HUMAN RACE!"

JESUS CONTINUES, "THERE ARE GOING TO BE TIMES, MY DEAR CHILD, THAT YOU WILL AGONIZE OVER WHAT YOU WANT AND WHAT YOUR HEAVENLY FATHER WANTS. HOWEVER, DOING WHAT HE WANTS CAN BRING ABOUT MIRACLES. (PAUSE)

"WHEN I GAVE UP MY WILL AND EMBRACED MY FATHER'S WILL, THE WHOLE HUMAN RACE WAS SAVED. DURING THESE TIMES OF AGONY PRAY TO MY FATHER FOR THE COURAGE AND FAITH NEEDED TO DO HIS WILL. HE WILL GIVE YOU ALL THAT YOU NEED."

YOU ASK JESUS, "HOW DO I KNOW WHAT GOD'S WILL IS FOR ME?

JESUS RESPONDS, "HE WILL SHOW YOU IN MANY WAYS. PRAY TO THE HOLY SPIRIT WHEN YOU THINK GOD IS

CALLING YOU TO DO SOMETHING. THE HOLY SPIRIT WILL ENLIGHTEN YOU. TRUST HIM AND FOLLOW HIM."

YOU SAY, "DEAR JESUS, I AM SO SORRY FOR MY SINS THAT CAUSED YOU TO SUFFER SUCH A HORRIBLE DEATH. I THANK YOU FOR DOING WHAT YOUR FATHER ASKED OF YOU. I THANK YOU FOR SAVING ME. I WILL PUT MY TRUST IN THE HOLY SPIRIT AND ASK HIM TO INSPIRE ME TO KNOW GOD'S WILL AND THEN TO FOLLOW IT."

JESUS SAYS, "THANK YOU FOR LISTENING TO ME AND NOT FALLING ASLEEP! I WILL CONTINUE BEING WITH YOU ON YOUR FAITH JOURNEY. ALL YOU HAVE TO DO IS TRUST IN ME. I LOVE YOU DEARLY, MY CHILD."

(SPEND A FEW MOMENTS IN SILENT PRAYER)

DISCUSSION GUIDE

1. HAVE YOU EVER AGONIZED OVER GIVING UP WHAT YOU WANT TO DO IN ORDER TO DO WHAT GOD WANTS YOU TO DO?

2. WHAT IS GOD'S WILL FOR YOU RIGHT NOW IN YOUR LIFE?

3. HAVE YOU EVER EXPERIENCED YOUR FRIENDS NOT BEING THERE FOR YOU? HOW DID YOU FEEL AT THOSE TIMES?

4. HAVE YOU EVER BEEN FRIGHTENED ABOUT SOMETHING YOU HAD TO FACE? HOW DID YOU DEAL WITH IT?

LENT: THE SCOURGING AT THE PILLAR

CLOSE YOUR EYES.

BREATHE IN, HOLD IT, BREATHE OUT. (3 TIMES)

YOU ARE STANDING IN A ROMAN COURTYARD, AND YOU SEE JESUS BEING HUMILIATED AS THE SOLDIERS STRIP HIM OF HIS CLOTHING AND TIE HIS HANDS TO A PILLAR. THE SOLDIERS ARE WHIPPING JESUS, AND YOU SEE HIS PRECIOUS BLOOD BEING POURED OUT FOR YOU. (PAUSE) JESUS IS IN IMMENSE PAIN BUT DOES NOT UTTER A SINGLE CRY. HE KNOWS THE PAIN HE IS SUFFERING IS NECESSARY FOR OUR SALVATION, AND HE IS WILLING TO GO THROUGH IT OUT OF HIS ABUNDANT LOVE FOR US. (PAUSE)

JESUS SUFFERED ALL THAT WE WILL EVER SUFFER -- LONELINESS, BETRAYAL, HUMILIATION, AND PAIN ARE JUST A FEW. (PAUSE) HE WAS ABANDONED BY HIS APOSTLES, BETRAYED BY ONE OF THEM, AND SUFFERED HUMILIATION AND EXCRUCIATING PAIN FOR US.

THERE ARE TIMES WHEN WE ARE LONELY, WHEN WE FEEL NOBODY CARES ABOUT US, AND WE HAVE NO ONE TO TURN TO. (PAUSE) AT THESE TIMES, ALL WE NEED TO DO IS REALIZE THAT CHRIST IS ALWAYS WITH US. HE

WILL NEVER ABANDON US. HE ALWAYS CARES ABOUT
US AND FOR US.

THERE ARE TIMES WHEN WE FEEL WE HAVE BEEN
BETRAYED BY OUR FRIENDS. WE MAY HAVE CONFIDED
A SECRET IN THEM AND THEY BETRAY US AND SPREAD
THE SECRET. (PAUSE) OFFER UP THE PAIN OF BETRAYAL
TO CHRIST WHO KNOWS HOW YOU FEEL. (PAUSE)

THERE ARE TIMES WHEN WE SUFFER HUMILITATION,
TOO, JUST AS JESUS DID. OUR PRIDE IS HURT, AND WE
JUST WANT TO RUN AWAY. YOU CAN USE THESE TIMES
TO OVERCOME THE SIN OF PRIDE AND GROW IN THE
VIRTUE OF HUMILITY. HUMILITY IS RECOGNIZING WHO
YOU ARE IN THE EYES OF GOD INSTEAD OF IN THE EYES
OF HUMANS. (PAUSE)

THERE ARE TIMES WHEN WE SUFFER PHYSICAL PAIN.
WOULD JESUS ASK US TO SUFFER MORE PAIN THAN WE
CAN HANDLE? THE ANSWER IS NO. HE SAID IN HIS OWN
WORDS, "I WILL NEVER GIVE YOU A CROSS TOO HEAVY
TO BEAR." (PAUSE)

IF WE RELY ON HIM TO HELP US CARRY OUR CROSSES,
HE WILL CERTAINLY HELP US. WHEN YOU ARE IN PAIN,
WHETHER IT BE PHYSICAL, EMOTIONAL, INTELLECTUAL
OR SPIRITUAL, UNITE YOUR PAIN WITH THE PAIN CHRIST
SUFFERED FOR YOU AND OFFER IT TO HIM AS A GIFT OF
YOUR LOVE . (PAUSE)

YOU STAND BEFORE CHRIST SHEDDING TEARS OF SORROW
FOR YOUR SINS AND TEARS OF JOY FOR HIS SAVING ACT
OF LOVE. (PAUSE)

(SPEND A FEW MOMENTS IN SILENT PRAYER.)

DISCUSSION GUIDE

1. WHO WOULD LIKE TO SHARE A TIME WHEN YOU EXPERIENCED LONELINESS?

2. WHO WOULD LIKE TO SHARE A TIME WHEN YOU FELT BETRAYED?

3. WHO WOULD LIKE TO SHARE A TIME WHEN YOU WERE HUMILIATED?

4. WHO WOULD LIKE TO SHARE A TIME WHEN YOU EXPERIENCED PAIN?

--physically --emotionally --intellectually --spiritually

LENT: THE CROWNING
WITH THORNS

CLOSE YOUR EYES.

BREATHE IN, HOLD IT, BREATHE OUT. (3 TIMES)

PICTURE YOURSELF STANDING IN THE ROMAN COURTYARD. (PAUSE) THE SOLDIERS THROW A PURPLE CLOAK AROUND JESUS. THEY PLACE A CROWN OF THORNS ON HIS HEAD AND A REED IN HIS RIGHT HAND. THEY THEN KNEEL DOWN BEFORE HIM AND MOCK HIM SAYING, "HAIL, KING OF THE JEWS!" THEY SPIT ON HIM AND KEEP STRIKING HIM ON THE HEAD WITH THE REED. THEY LAUGH AT HIM OUT LOUD. (PAUSE)

PURPLE WAS A SYMBOL OF ROYALTY. LITTLE DID THE SOLDIERS KNOW ABOUT THE ROYALTY OF JESUS, THE KING OF THE WHOLE HUMAN RACE! (PAUSE) WE ARE THE SERVANTS OF HIS KINGDOM. SERVANTS ARE FAITHFUL TO THEIR KING AND CARRY OUT HIS WISHES. (PAUSE) JESUS WISHES FOR US TO SPREAD THE GOOD NEWS OF HIS UNCONDITIONAL LOVE AND FORGIVENESS. (PAUSE) HE ASKS US TO LOVE AND FORGIVE ONE ANOTHER, TOO.

ALTHOUGH JESUS IS OUR KING, HE WASN'T CROWNED WITH A GOLD AND JEWELED CROWN. IT WAS A CROWN OF THORNS. JESUS NEVER DESIRED TO BE AN EARTHLY KING. HE IS OUR HEAVENLY KING. (PAUSE) EARTHLY

KINGDOMS DO NOT LAST, BUT HIS HEAVENLY KINGDOM IS EVERLASTING! (PAUSE)

WHAT IS A REED, AND WHY DID THE SOLDIERS PLACE IT IN JESUS' HAND? A REED IS A STRAIGHT STALK OF TALL GRASS THAT GROWS IN MARSHY PLACES. BECAUSE THEY ARE EASILY BLOWN FLAT BY THE WIND, THEY ARE SYMBOLIC OF WEAKNESS AND FICKLENESS. FICKLENESS MEANS "LIKELY TO CHANGE." (PAUSE) JESUS WAS NEITHER WEAK NOR FICKLE. HOW CAN THE SACRIFICE OF HIS LIFE FOR OUR SALVATION EVER BE CONSIDERED A SIGN OF WEAKNESS? (PAUSE) AND HIS TEACHINGS NEVER CHANGED. THEY ARE AS POWERFUL AND UNCHANGING TODAY AS THEY WERE TWO THOUSAND YEARS AGO. (PAUSE) WE ARE THE ONES WHO MUST CHANGE AND LIVE OUR LIVES ACCORDING TO HIS TEACHINGS. (PAUSE) LET US BE OPEN TO RECEIVE HIS PROCLAMATION OF LOVE AND FORGIVENESS AND THANK HIM FOR GIVING UP HIS LIFE FOR OUR SALVATION. (PAUSE)

LET US PRAY THAT WE WILL BE HIS FAITHFUL SERVANTS AND CARRY OUT HIS WILL FOR US. LET US TOGETHER ADORE, PRAISE, AND THANK OUR HEAVENLY KING!

(SPEND A FEW MOMENTS IN SILENT PRAYER.)

DISCUSSION GUIDE

1. IN WHAT WAYS CAN YOU SPREAD THE LOVE OF CHRIST?

2. IN WHAT WAYS CAN YOU SPREAD HIS FORGIVENESS?

3. THINK OF SOME AREAS IN WHICH YOU SHOW WEAKNESS. (HAVE STUDENTS THINK ABOUT THESE QUIETLY.)

4. THINK OF WAYS YOU CAN IMPROVE AND BECOME STRONGER. (HAVE STUDENTS THINK ABOUT THESE QUIETLY.)

LENT: JESUS CARRIES HIS CROSS

CLOSE YOUR EYES.

BREATHE IN, HOLD IT, BREATHE OUT (3 TIMES)

PICTURE YOURSELF WALKING WITH CHRIST ON THE WAY TO CALVARY. CHRIST HAS OPENLY ACCEPTED THE WOODEN CROSS, WHICH HE WILL CARRY AND ULTIMATELY BE NAILED UPON. (PAUSE)

YOU SEE HIM FALL THE FIRST TIME. HE IS BURDENED WITH ALL OF OUR SINS. (PAUSE) HE KNOWS THERE WILL BE TIMES THAT WE FALL TOO. HE ASKS US AT THESE TIMES TO REMEMBER HIS FALL, TURN TO HIM FOR HELP, AND GET UP AND CONTINUE GOING ON. (PAUSE)

ALONG THE WAY JESUS MEETS HIS MOTHER FACE TO FACE. HE SEES HER SUFFERING WITH HIM, LOVING HIM, AND SUPPORTING HIM IN CARRYING OUT THE WILL OF HIS FATHER -- TO SAVE ALL MANKIND. (PAUSE) NO WORDS ARE UTTERED BETWEEN THEM. NO WORDS ARE NECESSARY. THEY BOTH KNOW THIS IS WHAT THEY WERE BORN TO DO. (PAUSE)

JESUS IS STOPPED BY VERONICA WHO HAS COMPASSION FOR HIM AND WIPES THE BLOOD AND DIRT OFF HIS FACE WITH A MOIST CLOTH. (PAUSE) IN GRATITUDE FOR HER COMPASSIONATE ACT, HE LEAVES THE IMPRINT OF

HIS FACE ON THE CLOTH. EVEN DURING HIS INTENSE SUFFERING, HE LEAVES HIS MARK OF LOVE. (PAUSE)

YOU SEE JESUS FALL IN THE DUST A SECOND TIME, LYING UDER THE CRUSHING WEIGHT OF HIS CROSS. (PAUSE) EVERY TIME WE HELP SOMEONE ELSE CARRY THEIR BURDEN, WHETHER THEY ARE RICH, POOR, LONELY, SICK, OR DYING, WE ARE HELPING CHRIST TO GET ON HIS FEET AGAIN. (PAUSE)

JESUS FORGES ON AND MEETS THE WOMEN OF JERUSALEM WEEPING ALOUD FOR HIM. HE LOOKS AT THEM AND SAYS, "DAUGHTERS OF JERUSALEM, DO NOT WEEP FOR ME; WEEP INSTEAD FOR YOURSELVES AND FOR YOUR CHILDREN." JESUS IS LOOKING AHEAD TO THE DESTRUCTION OF ROME WHICH HAD SO MANY TIMES BEFORE, AND NOW FINALLY, REFUSED THE INVITATION OF GOD. (PAUSE) HE IS TELLING THESE WOMEN THAT IF THIS CITY COULD DO THIS TO HIM, WHO IS INNOCENT, WHAT MIGHT THEY DO TO THOSE WHO ARE GUILTY? (PAUSE)

YOU SEE JESUS FALL TO THE GROUND A THIRD TIME. (PAUSE) THE ROMAN SOLDIERS GRAB A MAN NAMED SIMON OF CYRENE TO HELP JESUS CARRY HIS CROSS TO THE HILL OF CALVARY. JUST AS JESUS ACCEPTS SIMON'S HELP, HE WANTS US TO ALLOW OTHERS TO HELP US CARRY OUR CROSSES. (PAUSE) WE MUST PUT ASIDE THE SIN OF PRIDE, GRASP THE VIRTUE OF HUMILITY, AND ACCEPT THE HELP OF OTHERS. JESUS DID! (PAUSE)

YOU PONDER ON ALL YOU HAVE SEEN AND HEARD. (PAUSE) YOU TELL JESUS YOU ARE SORRY FOR ALL YOUR SINS AND ASK HIM TO FORGIVE YOU. (PAUSE) YOU THANK HIM FOR SACRIFICING HIS LIFE TO SAVE YOU. (PAUSE) YOU ASK HIM TO HELP YOU BEAR YOUR CROSSES WITH LOVE AND PATIENCE.

(SPEND A FEW MOMENTS IN SILENT PRAYER.)

DISCUSSION GUIDE

1. WHAT ARE SOME CROSSES CHRIST MIGHT ASK YOU TO BEAR?

2. HOW CAN OUR MOTHER MARY HELP US CARRY OUR CROSSES?

3. HOW CAN YOU SHOW COMPASSION FOR OTHERS?

4. HOW CAN YOU HELP OTHERS CARRY THEIR CROSSES?

5. HOW CAN THE CROSSES GOD GIVES US HELP US TO BECOME MORE LIKE HIM?

POSSIBLE ANSWERS

---If we accept them with faith in God, He will help us.

---If we offer them up out of love for Him, He will bring us closer to Him.

---If we bear them patiently, He will heal our wound.

HOLY WEEK: HOLY THURSDAY

CLOSE YOUR EYES.

BREATHE IN, HOLD IT, BREATHE OUT. (3 TIMES)

YOU ARE IN THE UPPER ROOM WITH JESUS AND HIS APOSTLES WHO ARE CELEBRATING THE PASSOVER MEAL. IT IS HOLY THURSDAY AND JESUS IS SHARING HIS LAST MEAL WITH THEM. (PAUSE) "JESUS KNEW THAT HIS HOUR HAD COME TO PASS FROM THIS WORLD TO THE FATHER. HE LOVED HIS OWN IN THE WORLD, AND HE LOVED THEM TO THE END" (JOHN 13: 1). DURING THE SUPPER JESUS ROSE AND TOOK OFF HIS OUTER GARMENTS. HE TOOK A TOWEL AND TIED IT AROUND HIS WAIST. THEN HE POURED WATER INTO A BASIN AND BEGAN TO WASH THE DISCIPLES' FEET AND DRY THEM WITH THE TOWEL (JOHN 13: 4-6). JESUS SAID, "I HAVE GIVEN YOU A MODEL TO FOLLOW, SO THAT AS I HAVE DONE FOR YOU, YOU SHOULD ALSO DO" (JOHN: 15). JESUS WAS CALLING THEM TO SERVE OTHERS JUST AS HE DID, AND HE IS CALLING US TO DO THE SAME. (PAUSE)

THIS IS ALSO THE NIGHT THAT JESUS GAVE HIMSELF TO US IN THE AWESOME GIFT OF THE EUCHARIST AT THIS VERY FIRST MASS. THESE ARE THE WORDS IN LUKE'S GOSPEL. "THEN HE TOOK THE BREAD, SAID THE BLESSING, BROKE IT, AND GAVE IT TO THEM, SAYING, 'THIS IS MY BODY, WHICH WILL BE GIVEN FOR YOU; DO THIS IN MEMORY OF ME. AND LIKEWISE THE CUP AFTER THEY

HAD EATEN, SAYING, 'THIS CUP IS THE NEW COVENANT IN MY BLOOD,WHICH WILL BE SHED FOR YOU' " (LUKE 22: 19-21). (PAUSE) WHEN CHRIST SAID THE WORDS, "DO THIS IN MEMORY OF ME," HE INSTITUTED THE SACRAMENT OF THE PRIESTHOOD. THE LAST SUPPER WAS ALSO CHRIST'S FAREWELL TO HIS ASSEMBLED DISCIPLES, SOME OF WHOM WOULD BETRAY, DESERT, OR DENY HIM BEFORE THE SUN ROSE AGAIN. (PAUSE)

ON HOLY THURSDAY MORNING, THERE IS A SPECIAL MASS IN CATHEDRAL CHURCHES, CELEBRATED BY THE BISHOP AND AS MANY PRIESTS OF THE DIOCESE AS CAN ATTEND, BECAUSE IT IS A SOLEMN OBSERVANCE OF CHRIST'S INSTITUTION OF THE PRIESTHOOD AT THE LAST SUPPER. AT THIS "CHRISM MASS" THE BISHOP ALSO BLESSES THE OIL OF CHRISM USED FOR BAPTISM, CONFIRMATION AND ANOINTING OF THE SICK OR DYING. THE BISHOP MAY WASH THE FEET OF TWELVE OF THE PRIESTS, TO SYMBOLIZE CHRIST'S WASHING THE FEET OF HIS APOSTLES, THE FIRST PRIESTS.

BOYS, HAVE YOU EVER ASKED YOURSELF IF CHRIST IS CALLING YOU TO BE A PRIEST? (PAUSE) IF YOU FEEL HE IS CALLING YOU, THEN YOU NEED TO PRAY THAT HIS GRACE WILL LEAD YOU TO FOLLOW HIS CALL. (PAUSE) GIRLS, HAVE YOU EVER HEARD GOD CALLING YOU TO DEDICATE YOUR LIFE THROUGH ENTERING RELIGIOUS LIFE? IF YOU HAVE, PRAY YOU WILL HAVE THE COURAGE TO ANSWER THAT CALL. (PAUSE)

(SPEND A FEW MOMENTS IN SILENT PRAYER.)

DISCUSSION GUIDE

1. NAME SOME WAYS WE CAN BE SERVANTS TO OTHERS?

2. WHEN YOU RECEIVE CHRIST IN THE EUCHARIST DO YOU WELCOME HIM WITH LOVE AND TALK TO HIM? (reflect on this silently)

3. DO YOU FEEL CHRIST IS CALLING YOU TO RELIGIOUS LIFE?

4. DISCUSS WAYS THE MASS CAN BE MORE MEANINGFUL.

POSSIBLE ANSWERS

--listen for Christ's message to you in the readings

--offer Him your gifts and talents at the offertory and ask Him to help you use them in your life for His greater honor and glory

--listen to the prayers and words of the songs for His message

--receive Him in the Eucharist with love and gratitude

HOLY WEEK: GOOD FRIDAY

CLOSE YOUR EYES.

BREATHE IN, HOLD IT, BREATHE OUT. (3 TIMES)

PICTURE YOURSELF STANDING ON THE HILL OF CALVARY SEEING JESUS BEING NAILED TO THE CROSS. (PAUSE) HIS PRECIOUS HANDS THAT HEALED AND SERVED OTHERS ARE BEING NAILED TO THE CROSS. HIS PRECIOUS FEET WHICH TOOK HIM ON HIS JOURNEY TO TEACH OTHERS ARE BEING NAILED TO THE CROSS. (PAUSE) HE SILENTLY ACCEPTS THIS EXCRUCIATING PAIN OUT OF HIS BOUNDLESS LOVE FOR US. (PAUSE)

JESUS IS BEING CRUCIFIED ALONG WITH TWO CRIMINALS -- ONE ON HIS RIGHT AND THE OTHER ON HIS LEFT. DISMAS, A THIEF, WAS ONE OF THE CRIMINALS. HE REPENTED OF HIS SINS AND ASKED, "JESUS, REMEMBER ME WHEN YOU COME INTO YOUR KINGDOM." (LUKE 24: 42) JESUS SAID TO DISMAS, "AMEN, I SAY TO YOU, TODAY YOU WILL BE WITH ME IN PARADISE" (LUKE 24:43). THAT DAY DISMAS BECAME A SAINT! (PAUSE)

YOU HEAR JESUS SAY THE ASTOUNDING WORDS, "FATHER, FORGIVE THEM, THEY KNOW NOT WHAT THEY DO." IN THESE WORDS WE HEAR CHRIST FORGIVING ALL OF US BECAUSE WE KNOW NOT WHAT WE DO TO HIM EITHER. (PAUSE) FOR ALL THE TIMES WE HURT CHRIST WHO ABIDES IN OTHERS, FOR ALL THE TIMES WE FAIL

TO OBEY AND SERVE HIM, FOR ALL THE TIMES WE HAVE NEGLECTED TO COME TO HIM IN PRAYER, HE FORGIVES US. (PAUSE) WE NEED TO THANK HIM FOR HIS GREAT GIFT OF FORGIVENESS. (Reader says, "Let us silently thank Him now.")

JESUS' MOTHER AND HIS APOSTLE, JOHN, ARE STANDING BELOW JESUS.

JESUS SAYS TO MARY, "WOMAN, THIS IS YOUR SON." HE THEN SAID TO JOHN, "THIS IS YOUR MOTHER." WITH THESE WORDS, CHRIST GAVE ALL OF US THE PRECIOUS GIFT OF HIS LOVING MOTHER. (PAUSE) JUST AS SHE FOLLOWED HIM FROM HIS BIRTH TO DEATH, SHE IS WITH US ON OUR JOURNEY FROM BIRTH TO DEATH TOO. ALL WE NEED TO DO IS EMBRACE HER WITH LOVING ARMS AND TRUST IN HER TO LEAD US TO HER DIVINE SON. (PAUSE)

ON TOP OF ALL CHRIST'S SUFFERING, HE HAS NEVER **FELT** SO LONELY. HE CRIES OUT, "MY GOD, MY GOD, WHY HAVE YOU FORSAKEN ME?" (MARK 15:34) AT THIS TIME, HE **FEELS** THAT EVEN HIS FATHER HAS ABANDONED HIM. (PAUSE) THESE WERE HIS **FEELINGS**. IN REALITY, HIS FATHER DID NOT ABANDON HIM. HIS FATHER WELCOMED HIS SON BACK TO HIS HEAVENLY HOME. (PAUSE)

IN OUR TIMES OF LOSS, DON'T WE FEEL GOD HAS ABANDONED US? IN REALITY HE NEVER WILL. IF WE TRUST IN HIM AND ASK FOR HIS HELP, HE WILL HEAL OUR WOUNDS AND RESTORE OUR JOY. (PAUSE)

YOU ARE NOW SEEING JESUS IN HIS LAST MOMENT OF LIFE. HE CRIES OUT IN A LOUD VOICE, "FATHER, INTO YOUR HANDS I COMMEND MY SPIRIT" (LUKE 23:46). WHEN HE HAD SAID THIS HE BREATHED HIS LAST BREATH. (PAUSE) LET US SPEND A MOMENT IN SILENCE.

THE CENTURION WHO WITNESSED WHAT HAD HAPPENED GLORIFIED GOD AND SAID, "THIS MAN WAS INNOCENT BEYOND DOUBT" (LUKE 24:47). (PAUSE) WE ARE THE GUILTY ONES - GUILTY OF SIN. IF IT HADN'T BEEN FOR CHRIST'S DEATH WE WOULD HAVE NEVER BEEN SAVED. WHAT A GLORIOUS GIFT! THE GIFT OF HIS PRECIOUS LIFE! AND GOD CONTINUES TO HAVE MERCY ON US.

(SPEND A FEW MOMENTS IN SILENT PRAYER.)

DISCUSSION GUIDE

1. HOW CAN WE USE OUR HANDS AND FEET TO SERVE GOD?

2. DO YOU THINK BAD PEOPLE CAN GO TO HEAVEN?

3. ARE WE WILLING TO FORGIVE OTHERS? (SILENT REFLECTION)

4. HOW CAN YOU HONOR OUR MOTHER MARY?

5. NAME SOME TIMES WHEN YOU FELT LONELY.

EASTER: THE RESURRECTION

CLOSE YOUR EYES.

BREATHE IN, HOLD IT, BREATHE OUT. (3 TIMES)

IT IS THE MORNING OF CHRIST'S RESURRECTION FROM THE DEAD. YOU ARE STANDING OUTSIDE OF HIS TOMB. (PAUSE) ALL OF A SUDDEN YOU SEE THE HUGE STONE ROLL AWAY FROM THE ENTRANCE OF THE TOMB, AND RIGHT BEFORE YOUR VERY EYES, YOU SEE THE RESURRECTED CHRIST COMING OUT! (PAUSE) FROM THIS DAY FORWARD ALL OF LIFE IS NOW A CELEBRATION OF OUR SALVATION!

THE FIRST PERSON JESUS APPEARED TO WAS MARY MAGDALEN, WHO WAS OUTSIDE THE EMPTY TOMB WEEPING. (PAUSE) JESUS SAID TO HER, "WOMAN, WHY ARE YOU WEEPING? WHOM ARE YOU LOOKING FOR?"

SHE THOUGHT IT WAS THE GARDENER AND SAID TO HIM, "SIR, IF YOU CARRIED HIM AWAY, TELL ME WHERE YOU LAID HIM, AND I WILL TAKE HIM."

JESUS SAID TO HER, "MARY!"

SHE TURNED AND SAID TO HIM IN HEBREW, "RABBOUNI," WHICH MEANS TEACHER (JOHN 20: 15-17). IT WAS WHEN CHRIST CALLED HER BY NAME THAT SHE RECOGNIZED HIM AND WAS FILLED WITH JOY. (PAUSE) JESUS CALLS US BY NAME EACH DAY TO LIVE OUR LIVES IN HIM AND FOR

HIM. JUST AS HIS SUFFERING AND DEATH BROUGHT US THE JOY OF SALVATION, SO TOO, WILL OUR SUFFERING WITH CHRIST AND OUR LOVE FOR HIM BRING US JOY. (PAUSE)

JUST AS MARY MAGDALEN WAS WEEPING BECAUSE SHE DID NOT KNOW WHERE CHRIST WAS, SO TOO, WE FEEL LOST WITHOUT HIM IN OUR LIFE. MARY MAGDALEN EXPERIENCED JOY ONCE SHE RECOGNIZED CHRIST, AND SO WILL WE. HE APPEARS TO US IN MANY WAYS EACH DAY. WE CAN FIND HIM IN PRAYER, IN OTHERS, AND IN CREATION, BUT MOST OF ALL, IN THE EUCHARIST. (PAUSE) ON THE DAYS YOU DO NOT RECEIVE HIM IN THE EUCHARIST, YOU CAN HAVE A SPIRITUAL COMMUNION. JUST ASK JESUS TO COME TO YOU SPIRITUALLY AND HE WILL. (PAUSE)

ONCE MARY MAGDALEN RECOGNIZED JESUS, HE SAID TO HER, "GO TO MY BROTHERS AND TELL THEM, 'I AM GOING TO MY FATHER AND YOUR FATHER, TO MY GOD AND YOUR GOD.'"

WITH THESE WORDS, JESUS TOLD US HIS FATHER IS OUR FATHER, WHICH MAKES US ALL HIS SONS AND DAUGHTERS FOREVER. LET US LIVE OUR LIVES AS CHILDREN OF THE LORD. (PAUSE)

ON THE EVENING OF THAT FIRST DAY OF THE WEEK, THE DISCIPLES WERE BEHIND LOCKED DOORS IN FEAR OF THE JEWS. JESUS CAME AND STOOD IN THEIR MIDST AND SAID TO THEM, "PEACE BE WITH YOU." WHEN HE HAD SAID THIS, HE SHOWED THEM HIS HANDS AND HIS SIDE. THE DISCIPLES REJOICED WHEN THEY SAW THE LORD. JESUS SAID TO THEM AGAIN, "PEACE BE WITH YOU. AS THE FATHER HAS SENT ME, SO I SEND YOU" (JOHN 20:19-21). WITH THESE WORDS, CHRIST COMMISSIONED HIS DISCIPLES TO CONTINUE HIS WORK IN THE WORLD. WE

ARE HIS DISCIPLES TODAY, AND HE ASKS US TO SPREAD HIS GOOD NEWS TO OTHERS TOO. (PAUSE) SHARE YOUR KNOWLEDGE AND LOVE FOR GOD WITH OTHERS: YOUR FAMILY, FRIENDS, AND CLASSMATES. FIND OTHERS WITH WHOM YOU CAN SHARE YOUR SPIRITUAL JOURNEY. A LIFE WITH CHRIST WILL BRING YOU PEACE. JUST AS HE SAID TO HIS APOSTLES, "PEACE BE WITH YOU," SO HE SAYS THESE WORDS TO EACH OF US. THAT IS WHAT HE WANTS FOR US, BUT WE WILL FIND IT ONLY IN HIM. (PAUSE)

THOMAS, CALLED DIDYMUS, ONE OF THE TWELVE, WAS NOT WITH THEM WHEN JESUS CAME. SO THE OTHER DISCIPLES SAID TO HIM, "WE HAVE SEEN THE LORD."

BUT THOMAS SAID TO THEM, "UNLESS I SEE THE MARK OF THE NAILS IN HIS HANDS AND PUT MY FINGER INTO THE NAILMARKS AND PUT MY HAND INTO HIS SIDE, I WILL NOT BELIEVE."

NOW A WEEK LATER HIS DISCIPLES WERE AGAIN INSIDE, AND THOMAS WAS WITH THEM. JESUS CAME, ALTHOUGH THE DOORS WERE LOCKED, AND STOOD IN THEIR MIDST AND SAID, "PEACE BE WITH YOU." THEN HE SAID TO THOMAS, "PUT YOUR FINGER HERE AND SEE MY HANDS, AND BRING YOUR HAND AND PUT IT INTO MY SIDE, AND DO NOT BE UNBELIEVING, BUT BELIEVE."

THOMAS ANSWERED AND SAID TO HIM, "MY LORD AND MY GOD!"

JESUS SAID TO HIM, "HAVE YOU COME TO BELIEVE BECAUSE YOU HAVE SEEN ME? BLESSED ARE THOSE WHO HAVE NOT SEEN AND HAVE BELIEVED." (JOHN 20:24-29)

WHAT JESUS MEANT WAS THAT THOSE OF US WHO BELIEVE AND HAVE NOT SEEN ARE BLESSED! WE ARE BLESSED WITH THE GIFT OF OUR FAITH IN HIM. (PAUSE)

LET US CELEBRATE CHRIST'S RESURRECTION EVERY DAY AND ESPECIALLY AT EVERY MASS. (PAUSE)

(SPEND A FEW MOMENTS IN SILENT PRAYER.)

DISCUSSION GUIDE

1. HOW CAN OUR SUFFERING BRING US CLOSER TO GOD?

2. DO WE RECOGNIZE CHRIST WHEN HE CALLS US TO DO HIS WILL?

3. HOW CAN WE DEEPEN OUR FAITH IN GOD EACH DAY?

4. HOW CAN WE CELEBRATE OUR LIFE?

--come closer to Christ in prayer

--make Christ number one in your life

--live your life doing God's will just as Christ did

--celebrate the gift of others in your life

APRIL: WEEK 2 -
JUSTICE AND PEACE

CLOSE YOUR EYES.

BREATHE IN, HOLD IT, BREATHE OUT (3 TIMES)

YOU AND JESUS ARE STANDING IN A HALL OF JUSTICE. HE POINTS OUT A PICTURE OF A SCALE TO YOU -- A SYMBOL OF JUSTICE. (PAUSE)

JESUS LOOKS AT YOU AND SAYS, "I HAVE CALLED ALL PEOPLE TO BE JUST. BEING A JUST PERSON MEANS YOU TREAT ME AND ONE ANOTHER FAIRLY. I KNOW YOU ARE WONDERING HOW YOU CAN TREAT ME FAIRLY. WHEN YOU TREAT OTHERS FAIRLY, YOU ARE ALSO TREATING ME IN THAT WAY. (PAUSE) NOW YOU ARE WONDERING HOW YOU CAN TREAT OTHERS FAIRLY. LET'S TAKE A LOOK AT YOUR FAMILY AND FRIENDS, AND LET US NOT FORGET THE POOR AND LONELY."

JESUS ASKS, "DO YOU TREAT THE MEMBERS OF YOUR FAMILY FAIRLY? DO YOU PRAY WITH THEM? (PAUSE) DO YOU DO YOUR PART IN THE FAMILY CHORES? (SILENT REFLECTION) DO YOU THANK YOUR PARENTS FOR ALL THEY DO FOR YOU? (SILENT REFLECTION) DO YOU HELP YOUR BROTHERS AND/OR SISTERS? (SILENT REFLECTION) THESE ARE JUST A FEW WAYS OF TREATING YOUR FAMILY JUSTLY. I'M SURE YOU CAN THINK OF OTHER WAYS TOO."

(Say aloud to students, "Take time now to think of others ways to treat your family justly.")

JESUS ASKS, "ARE YOU TREATING YOUR FRIENDS FAIRLY? DO YOU LISTEN TO THEM WHEN THEY NEED YOU TO? (PAUSE) ARE YOU SPENDING TIME WITH THEM? (PAUSE) DO YOU SACRIFICE WHAT YOU WANT TO DO AND SHARE TIME DOING WHAT THEY LIKE TO DO? (PAUSE) CAN THEY TRUST YOU WITH THEIR SECRETS? (PAUSE) IN WHICH OF THESE AREAS CAN YOU IMPROVE YOUR FRIENDSHIP?" (Say aloud to students, "Take time now to think of ways you can improve.")

YOU RESPOND, "DEAR JESUS, I HAVEN'T BEEN THE BEST FAMILY MEMBER OR FRIEND I COULD BE. HELP ME BE THE KIND OF FRIEND THAT YOU ARE -- LOVING AND CONSIDERATE OF OTHERS' FEELINGS. YOU ARE A GREAT MODEL OF FRIENDSHIP, AND I WANT TO BE THE BEST FRIEND I CAN BE."

JESUS SAYS, "LET US NOT FORGET THE POOR AND LONELY. THERE ARE MANY WAYS YOU CAN TREAT THEM JUSTLY. YOU CAN HELP FEED AND CLOTHE THE POOR. I HAVE GIVEN THE WORLD ENOUGH FOOD TO FEED EVERYONE. IT IS THE GREED OF SOME PEOPLE THAT CAUSE OTHERS TO STARVE. THAT IS NOT JUST! SHARE SOME OF THE GIFTS I HAVE GIVEN YOU WITH THE POOR. (PAUSE) AND THE LONELY, VISIT THEM. HELP THEM WITH SOME OF THE CHORES THEY CAN NO LONGER DO. LEARN FROM THEIR WISDOM AND EXPERIENCE. THEY HAVE A LOT TO GIVE YOU IN RETURN. (PAUSE) TREATING OTHERS JUSTLY WILL BRING PEACE TO YOU AND OTHERS. THAT IS MY WILL."

YOU LOOK AT JESUS AND SAY, "DEAR JESUS, I WANT TO BE YOUR INSTRUMENT OF JUSTICE AND PEACE IN THE WORLD. I DO NOT HAVE TO LOOK FAR TO SEE YOU IN MY FAMILY, FRIENDS, AND THE POOR AND LONELY. GIVE

ME YOUR GRACE TO SHARE MY GIFTS WITH THEM AND MAKE A DIFFERENCE IN THEIR LIVES."

JESUS LOOKS AT YOU WITH LOVE IN HIS EYES AND SAYS, "DO ALL YOU CAN DO, MY CHILD, TO BRING PEACE AND JUSTICE TO OTHERS, AND I WILL BE AT YOUR SIDE WORKING THROUGH AND WITH YOU. PEACE BE WITH YOU."

(SPEND A FEW MOMENTS IN SILENT PRAYER.)

DISCUSSION GUIDE

1. HOW CAN YOU BRING PEACE AND JUSTICE TO YOUR FAMILY?

2. HOW CAN YOU BRING PEACE AND JUSTICE TO YOUR FRIENDS?

3. GIVE SOME EXAMPLES OF HOW YOU CAN HELP THE POOR.

   POSSIBLE ANSWERS

   ---donate food to the poor

   ---donate your used clothing to the poor

   ---spend some time in a soup kitchen serving the poor

4. GIVE SOME EXAMPLES OF HOW YOU CAN HELP THE LONELY.

POSSIBLE ANSWERS

---visit them

---help them with chores

---run errands for them

APRIL: WEEK 3 - KEEPING YOUR WORD

CLOSE YOUR EYES.

BREATHE IN, HOLD IT, BREATHE OUT (3 TIMES)

YOU AND JESUS ARE LOOKING AT THE BIBLE. HE SAYS, "YOU KNOW THE BIBLE CONTAINS MY HOLY WORD. IN THE WORDS OF THE OLD TESTAMENT, MY FATHER PROMISED HE WOULD SEND ME TO SAVE THE WORLD. MY FATHER KEPT HIS WORD. (PAUSE) IN THE WORDS OF THE NEW TESTAMENT, I SHOWED ALL MANKIND THAT I WAS THE WAY, THE TRUTH, AND THE LIFE. I LIVED MY LIFE ON EARTH KEEPING MY WORD ALWAYS. (PAUSE) I HAVE CALLED YOU TO DO THE SAME. KEEPING YOUR WORD IS SOMETIMES ALL YOU HAVE TO GIVE." (PAUSE)

JESUS CONTINUES, "WHEN YOU GIVE OTHERS YOUR WORD, THEY COUNT ON YOU TO KEEP IT TO THE BEST OF YOUR ABILITY. (PAUSE) GIVING YOUR WORD IS A VALUABLE GIFT TO OTHERS. CAN PEOPLE COUNT ON YOU TO KEEP YOUR WORD? (Teacher says, "Silently reflect on this question.")

FURTHERMORE, JESUS SAYS, "JUST GIVING YOUR WORD IS NOT ENOUGH. YOU MUST CARRY OUT YOUR WORD. DO WHAT YOU PROMISED TO DO NO MATTER HOW INCONVENIENT IT MAY BE TO YOU. (PAUSE) CARRYING

OUT YOUR WORD SHOWS YOU ARE TRUSTWORTHY AND THAT YOU RESPECT OTHERS. WILL PEOPLE RESPECT YOU IF YOU KEEP YOUR WORD? YOU BET! IF YOU WANT THE RESPECT OF OTHERS, THEN RESPECT THEM BY KEEPING YOUR WORD."

FINALLY, JESUS SAYS, "FAILING TO KEEP YOUR WORD CAN CAUSE A LOT OF HURT IN OTHERS. DON'T GIVE YOUR WORD IF YOU CAN'T KEEP IT. (PAUSE) REMEMBER WHAT YOU DO TO OTHERS, YOU DO TO ME. I TRUST YOU DO NOT WANT TO HURT ME."

YOU ANSWER, "NO, DEAR LORD, I DO NOT WANT TO HURT YOU. I WANT TO SHOW YOU THAT YOU CAN COUNT ON ME TO KEEP MY WORD. I NOW KNOW THAT WHEN I GIVE MY WORD TO OTHERS, I AM REALLY GIVING IT TO YOU. PLEASE GIVE ME THE GRACE I NEED TO KEEP MY WORD."

JESUS REPLIES, "I WILL GIVE YOU THE GRACE YOU NEED. ALL YOU HAVE TO DO IS ACCEPT IT AND ALLOW ME TO WORK IN YOU. (PAUSE) I CONTINUE TO KEEP MY PROMISE TO YOU THAT I WILL ALWAYS LOVE YOU AND BE THERE FOR YOU. I GIVE YOU MY WORD, AND I AM COUNTING ON YOU TO KEEP YOUR WORD."

YOU REPLY, "YOU CAN COUNT ON ME, JESUS."

(SPEND A FEW MOMENTS IN SILENT PRAYER.)

DISCUSSION GUIDE

1. WHAT DOES IT MEAN TO KEEP YOUR WORD?

2. HOW DO YOU FEEL WHEN OTHERS DO NOT KEEP THEIR WORD?

3. WHEN YOU DO NOT KEEP YOUR WORD HOW DOES THAT AFFECT YOUR RELATIONSHIP WITH OTHERS? WITH GOD?

4. DO YOU THINK IT IS IMPORTANT TO KEEP YOUR WORD? WHY?

POSSIBLE ANSWERS

---When others can't trust you to keep your word they feel you are really lying to them

---If you want others to trust you then it is important to keep your word

MAY: WEEK 1 - OUR BLESSED MOTHER AND THE ROSARY

CLOSE YOUR EYES.

BREATHE IN, HOLD IT, BREATHE OUT. (3 TIMES)

YOU AND OUR BLESSED MOTHER ARE TAKING A WALK IN A BEAUTIFUL GARDEN FULL OF COLORFUL FLOWERS. SHE INVITES YOU TO SIT WITH HER AND ENJOY THE BEAUTY. (PAUSE)

SHE SAYS TO YOU, "YOU KNOW, WHEN I BECAME THE MOTHER OF JESUS I ALSO BECAME YOUR MOTHER. I LOVE YOU WITH ALL MY HEART AND WANT TO SEE YOU JOIN MY SON AND ME IN HEAVEN.

"I WOULD LIKE TO TALK TO YOU TODAY ABOUT THE IMPORTANCE OF SAYING THE ROSARY. IN 1917, BETWEEN THE MONTHS OF MAY AND OCTOBER, I APPEARED SIX TIMES TO THREE SHEPHERD CHILDREN NEAR THE TOWN OF FATIMA IN PORTUGAL. I PROMISED THAT HEAVEN WOULD GRANT PEACE TO ALL THE WORLD IF MY REQUESTS FOR PRAYER, REPARATION, AND CONSECRATION WERE HEARD AND OBEYED. I EMPHASIZED THE NECESSITY OF PRAYING THE ROSARY DAILY. THOSE THREE CHILDREN PASSED ON MY MESSAGE TO THE WORLD. I INVITE YOU TO DO THE SAME. (PAUSE)

WHEN SAYING THE ROSARY, YOU MEDITATE ON DIFFERENT MYSTERIES WHICH ARE SIGNIFICANT EVENTS IN THE LIVES OF MY SON AND ME. IN DOING SO, YOU WILL BECOME MORE AWARE OF THE LOVE GOD HAS FOR YOU. (PAUSE) I URGE YOU TO PRAY THE ROSARY AS OFTEN AS YOU CAN IF YOU CANNOT SAY IT DAILY. EVEN ONE DECADE A DAY WOULD BE MEANINGFUL. I INVITE YOU TO COME TO KNOW AND LOVE MY SON. HE WILL CHANGE YOUR LIFE FOREVER." (PAUSE)

YOU LOOK AT MARY AND SAY, "THANK YOU, DEAR MOTHER, FOR LOVING ME AND TELLING ME HOW TO COME CLOSER TO YOUR SON. I REALLY WANT TO BE MORE LIKE HIM AND GROW IN MY LOVE FOR HIM EACH DAY. I WILL TRY MY BEST TO SAY THE ROSARY AS OFTEN AS I CAN OR AT LEAST A DECADE A DAY. THANK YOU FOR BEING THE WONDERFUL MOTHER THAT YOU ARE." (PAUSE)

(SPEND A FEW MOMENTS IN SILENT PRAYER.)

(SPEND TIME EXPLAINING THE ROSARY AND THE MYSTERIES. TO GAIN ACCESS TO WEBSITES ON THIS INFORMATION, GOOGLE "HOW TO SAY THE ROSARY" AND "MYSTERIES OF THE ROSARY".)

DISCUSSION GUIDE

1. DO YOU HAVE ANY QUESTIONS ABOUT HOW TO SAY THE ROSARY?

2. WHY ARE THE MONTHS OF MAY AND OCTOBER DEDICATED TO MARY?

   --This was the period of time that Mary appeared to the children at Fatima.

3. DO YOU HAVE ANY KIND OF DEVOTION TO MARY?

4. HOW CAN YOU IMITATE OUR BLESSED MOTHER?

MAY: WEEK 2 - TRUSTING IN GOD'S WILL

CLOSE YOUR EYES.

BREATHE IN, HOLD IT, BREATHE OUT. (3 TIMES)

YOU AND JESUS ARE STANDING ON A CLIFF OVERLOOKING THE BEAUTIFUL BLUE OCEAN. THE SKY IS A BEAUTIFUL BLUE, AND THE SUN IS SHINING BRIGHTLY. (PAUSE) HE ASKS YOU, "DO YOU TRUST ME WITH YOUR LIFE?"

YOU ANSWER, "YOU KNOW, JESUS, THAT I AM LACKING IN MY TRUST IN YOU. I LIKE TO BE IN CONTROL OF MY OWN LIFE. HOW CAN I TRUST IN YOU MORE?" (PAUSE)

JESUS LOOKS IN YOUR EYES AND SAYS, "MY DEAR CHILD, I KNOW WHAT IS BEST FOR YOU, AND I LOVE YOU DEARLY, BUT IT IS YOUR CHOICE TO TRUST IN ME OR NOT. YOU CAN PLAN YOUR DAY, AND IF THINGS DON'T GO AS YOU PLANNED, JUST TRUST THAT WHAT I HAVE OFFERED YOU THAT DAY IS BETTER FOR YOU. RATHER THAN BEING DISAPPOINTED ACCEPT WHAT I HAVE OFFERED YOU INSTEAD. (PAUSE) DO NOT WORRY. WORRYING IS USELESS. TRUSTING IN ME WILL BRING YOU PEACE AND HAPPINESS. (PAUSE) I HAVE GIVEN YOU ALL THAT YOU NEED TO LIVE YOUR LIFE IN THE WAY I LIVED MINE -- DOING MY FATHER'S WILL. JUST AS I SERVED MANKIND I ASK THAT YOU DO THE SAME. REMEMBER THE TWO GREATEST COMMANDMENTS: LOVE GOD ABOVE ALL

ELSE AND YOUR NEIGHBOR AS YOURSELF. (PAUSE) BRING MY LOVE TO ALL THOSE YOU MEET EACH DAY. TRUST THAT LIVING YOUR LIFE ACCORDING TO THE FATHER'S WILL IS ALL HE IS ASKING OF YOU." (PAUSE)

YOU ASK JESUS, "HOW DO I KNOW IF I AM DOING THE FATHER'S WILL?"

JESUS SAYS, "ASK YOURSELF THESE THREE QUESTIONS: IS IT GOOD FOR GOD? IS IT GOOD FOR OTHERS? IS IT GOOD FOR YOURSELF? IF YOU CAN ANSWER 'YES' TO ALL THREE QUESTIONS, THEN YOU ARE DOING GOD'S WILL."

YOU LOOK BACK AT JESUS AND RESPOND, "JESUS, I WANT TO DO THE WILL OF THE FATHER. HELP ME TO PUT ASIDE MY SELFISHNESS AND SURRENDER MY WILL TO THE FATHER. THIS IS NOT GOING TO BE EASY, I KNOW, BUT I WILL WORK ON IT EVERY DAY. (PAUSE)

JESUS SAYS, "THAT IS ALL THE FATHER ASKS -- THAT YOU WORK AT IT EACH DAY. IT WASN'T EASY FOR ME EITHER. I DIDN'T WANT TO BE CRUCIFIED ON A CROSS; BUT IN SURRENDERING MY WILL TO MY FATHER, I SAVED YOU AND ALL THE REST OF MANKIND. I TRUSTED MY FATHER, AND BECAUSE I TRUSTED IN HIM, YOU ARE NOW FREE TO BE WITH ME IN HEAVEN IF THAT IS WHAT YOU CHOOSE." (PAUSE)

YOU REPLY, "DEAR JESUS, I TRUST THAT WHAT YOU ARE TELLING ME IS WHAT IS BEST FOR ME, AND I THANK YOU WITH ALL MY HEART. I LOVE YOU, DEAR JESUS, AND WANT TO BE YOUR FAITHFUL SERVANT IN THE WORLD."

JESUS TAKES YOUR HAND AND ASKS THAT YOU WALK WITH HIM EACH DAY OF YOUR LIFE.

(SPEND A FEW MOMENTS IN SILENT PRAYER.)

DISCUSSION GUIDE

1. HOW DO WE KNOW WE ARE DOING GOD'S WILL?

    Ask yourself these three questions.

    Is it good for God? Is it good for others? Is it good for myself?

2. HOW DID JESUS CARRY OUT THE WILL OF HIS FATHER?

3. HOW DID THE BLESSED VIRGIN CARRY OUT GOD'S WILL?

4. HOW DID THE SAINTS CARRY OUT GOD'S WILL?

MAY: WEEK 3 - HOW TO CHOOSE YOUR FRIENDS

CLOSE YOUR EYES.

BREATHE IN, HOLD IT, BREATHE OUT. (3 TIMES)

YOU AND JESUS ARE WALKING ON A PATH IN A GARDEN OF RED, PINK, AND YELLOW ROSES. (PAUSE) HE SAYS HE WANTS TO TALK TO YOU ABOUT HOW TO CHOOSE YOUR FRIENDS. YOU SAY, "DEAR JESUS, I WOULD LIKE TO HEAR YOUR ADVICE."

HE SAYS, "WHEN CHOOSING YOUR FRIENDS ASK YOURSELF THESE QUESTIONS: DO THEY SHARE MY FAITH IN GOD? DO THEY BRING ME CLOSER TO GOD? DO THEY SHARE MY VALUES AND RESPECT ME? IF YOU CAN ANSWER 'YES' TO THESE QUESTIONS, THEY ARE GOOD FRIENDS. (PAUSE) CHOOSING THESE KINDS OF FRIENDS WILL HELP YOU ON YOUR FAITH JOURNEY. DON'T ALLOW PEOPLE TO LEAD YOU DOWN THE PATH OF DESTRUCTION SUCH AS USING ILLEGAL DRUGS AND ALCOHOL. MOST OF ALL, BE TRUE TO ME AND YOURSELF. DOES THIS MAKE SENSE TO YOU?"

YOU LOOK AT JESUS AND SAY, "YES, LORD, IT DOES MAKE SENSE, BUT IT IS NOT ALWAYS EASY."

JESUS SAYS, "I KNOW THAT, MY CHILD. JUST REMEM-
BER THAT ONE OF MY FRIENDS BETRAYED ME. (PAUSE)
MAINTAINING FRIENDSHIPS TAKES A LOT OF WORK. YOU
HAVE TO LEARN TO GIVE WHAT YOU HAVE TO OFFER
AND TAKE WHAT THEY HAVE TO OFFER. THIS IS THE WAY
TRUE FRIENDSHIP BLOSSOMS. (PAUSE) I INVITE YOU TO
BE MY FRIEND. I HAVE A LOT TO OFFER YOU -- PEACE,
HAPPINESS, JOY, AND ETERNAL LIFE WITH ME IN HEAV-
EN. WOULD YOU BE MY FRIEND?"

"YES, LORD, I WANT YOU TO BE MY BEST FRIEND, AND I
WANT TO BE YOURS. I KNOW THAT FOLLOWING YOU IS
THE BEST CHOICE I CAN MAKE. PLEASE HELP ME TO BE
THE KIND OF FRIEND YOU WANT ME TO BE -- TO BRING
YOUR LOVE TO OTHERS. PLEASE GIVE ME THE GRACE TO
FORGIVE MY FRIENDS WHEN THEY HURT ME AND I ASK
THAT YOU HELP THEM TO FORGIVE ME WHEN I HURT
THEM."

JESUS RESPONDS, "THANK YOU FOR CHOOSING ME AS
YOUR BEST FRIEND. I WILL ALWAYS BE THERE FOR YOU.
YOU CAN COUNT ON THAT."

JESUS BENDS OVER AND PICKS A YELLOW ROSE, A
SYMBOL OF FRIENDSHIP, AND GIVES IT TO YOU WITH A
SMILE ON HIS FACE.

(SPEND A FEW MOMENTS IN SILENT PRAYER.)

DISCUSSION GUIDE

1. DO YOUR FRIENDS BRING YOU CLOSER TO GOD?

2. DO YOU AND YOUR FRIENDS SHARE YOUR FAITH JOURNEY?

3. DO YOUR FRIENDS RESPECT YOU?

4. WHAT ARE SOME THINGS YOU CAN SHARE WITH YOUR FRIENDS?

POSSIBLE ANSWERS

--your faith journey

--your gifts and talents

--your trust

--your time

MAY: WEEK 4 - BALANCE
IN YOUR LIFE

CLOSE YOUR EYES.

BREATHE IN, HOLD IT, BREATHE OUT (3 TIMES)

JESUS INVITES YOU TO GO FOR A WALK WITH HIM AND HIS MOTHER, MARY, IN A BEAUTIFUL GARDEN. IT IS ONLY THE THREE OF YOU THERE, AND IT IS VERY QUIET EXCEPT FOR THE SONGS OF THE BIRDS. HE INVITES YOU TO LOOK AT THE BEAUTIFUL TREES AND MULTI-COLORED FLOWERS THAT HE HAS CREATED FOR YOU. (PAUSE)

JESUS SAYS, "THIS IS YOUR LAST WEEK OF THIS SCHOOL YEAR, AND I AND MY MOTHER WOULD LIKE TO GIVE YOU SOME SUGGESTIONS FOR PLANNING YOUR SUMMER VACATION. WOULD YOU LIKE TO HEAR THEM?"

YOU ANSWER, "I AM ALL EARS, DEAR LORD."

JESUS BEGINS BY SAYING, "YOU MUST HAVE A BALANCE IN YOUR LIFE. THERE ARE FOUR THINGS I WOULD LIKE YOU TO DO EACH DAY. FIRST OF ALL, MAKE TIME FOR PRAYER WITH ME AND MY MOTHER. START YOUR DAY BY TELLING ME THAT EVERYTHING YOU DO THAT DAY YOU DO OUT OF YOUR LOVE FOR ME. THAT WAY YOUR WHOLE DAY IS A PRAYER. (PAUSE) I ALSO RECOMMEND YOU TO DO A FEW MINUTES OF SPIRITUAL READING WHICH WILL

HELP YOU COME TO KNOW AND LOVE ME MORE, AND TO BECOME A BETTER CHRISTIAN. (PAUSE) IN HONOR OF MY DEAR MOTHER PLEASE SAY A ROSARY EACH DAY OR AT LEAST ONE DECADE ASKING FOR WORLD PEACE."

MARY LOOKS AT YOU AND SAYS, "I WOULD LIKE YOU TO DO THAT AND I WILL ALSO BLESS YOU EACH DAY."

JESUS CONTINUES, "SECOND, I WOULD LIKE YOU TO SPEND QUALITY TIME WITH YOUR FAMILY AND FRIENDS EACH DAY. THEY ARE IMPORTANT IN YOUR LIFE AND THEY DESERVE TO HAVE SOME OF YOUR TIME. TELL THEM HOW MUCH YOU LOVE THEM AND HOW BLESSED YOU ARE TO HAVE THEM IN YOUR LIFE." (PAUSE)

MARY LOOKS AT YOU AND SAYS, "MY SON WOULD ALSO LIKE YOU TO SPEND TIME EACH DAY DOING SOMETHING FOR SOMEONE ELSE. HE HAS CALLED ALL OF US TO SERVE HIM IN OTHERS. REMEMBER, IT IS IN GIVING THAT YOU WILL RECEIVE."

"LAST, BUT NOT LEAST," JESUS SAYS, "I WANT YOU TO FIND TIME EACH DAY DOING WHAT YOU ENJOY MOST AS LONG AS IT IS NOT SINFUL. (PAUSE) IT IS IMPORTANT FOR YOU THAT YOU FIND HAPPINESS IN DOING WHAT YOU ENJOY. I HAVE GIVEN YOU THIS VACATION TO RESTORE YOUR SPIRITUAL LIFE, TO ENJOY YOUR RELATIONSHIPS WITH FAMILY AND FRIENDS, TO FIND TIME TO SERVE ME, TO REFRESH YOUR PHYSICAL BODY, AND TO HAVE FUN ENJOYING WHAT YOU LIKE TO DO. MAKE THE MOST OF THIS TIME AND LIVE YOUR SUMMER WITH JOY IN YOUR HEART."

YOU LOOK AT JESUS AND MARY AND SAY, "THANK YOU TO BOTH OF YOU FOR YOUR SUGGESTIONS IN HELPING ME PLAN MY SUMMER VACATION. WITH YOUR BLESSINGS I WILL TRY TO DO ALL YOU HAVE INVITED ME TO DO TO

MAKE IT PROFITABLE AND PLEASING TO BOTH OF YOU. THANK YOU FOR OUR WONDERFUL WALK AND TALK TIME. I LOVE YOU BOTH VERY MUCH AND WANT TO BE LIKE YOU."

JESUS AND MARY BOTH GIVE YOU THEIR BLESSING AND A BIG SMILE.

(SPEND A FEW MOMENTS IN SILENT PRAYER.)

DISCUSSION GUIDE

1. WHAT IS THE MOST IMPORTANT THING TO FIND TIME FOR EACH DAY?

2. WHY IS IT IMPORTANT TO SPEND QUALITY TIME WITH YOUR FAMILY AND FRIENDS?

3. NAME SOME WAYS YOU CAN SERVE OTHERS THIS SUMMER?

4. WHY IS IT IMPORTANT FOR YOU TO DO WHAT YOU ENJOY?

MEDITATION FOR GRADE 8 - GRADUATION

CLOSE YOUR EYES.

BREATHE IN, HOLD IT, BREATHE OUT (3 TIMES)

YOU ARE STANDING WITH JESUS AT THE BOTTOM OF A WHITE GRANITE STAIRWAY. AT THE TOP OF THIS STAIRWAY IS HIS HEAVENLY HOME WHERE YOU WILL JOIN HIM AFTER YOUR LIFE'S JOURNEY. (PAUSE) YOU AND JESUS, HAND IN HAND, HAVE ALREADY CLIMBED A FEW STEPS TOGETHER -- YOUR BIRTH, YOUR BAPTISM, YOUR FIRST HOLY COMMUNION, AND YOUR CATHOLIC ELEMENTARY EDUCATION. YOU ARE BOTH READY TO CLIMB THE NEXT STEP TOGETHER, GOING INTO HIGH SCHOOL. (PAUSE)

SOMETIMES GRADUATION IS CALLED "COMMENCEMENT," WHICH DOESN'T MEAN THE END OF SOMETHING. IT REALLY MEANS ANOTHER "BEGINNING." YOU ARE BEGINNING A FOUR-YEAR JOURNEY IN HIGH SCHOOL. IN THESE NEXT FOUR YEARS OF YOUR LIFE, YOU WILL BE PRESENTED WITH MANY OPPORTUNITIES. YOU WILL ALSO HAVE TO MAKE GOOD CHOICES THAT WILL ENABLE YOU TO SERVE THE LORD THE BEST YOU CAN. (PAUSE)

YOU WILL HAVE THE OPPORTUNITY TO MAKE MORE FRIENDS, AND TO LEARN ALL YOU CAN IN ORDER TO SOME DAY DO WHAT IT IS GOD IS CALLING YOU TO DO:

TO SERVE HIS PEOPLE AND TO GROW IN YOUR SPIRITUAL LIFE. ALWAYS REMEMBER TO PUT GOD FIRST IN YOUR LIFE, OTHERS SECOND, AND YOURSELF THIRD. (PAUSE)

YOU WILL BE CONFRONTED WITH MANY TEMPTATIONS TO ENGAGE IN SEX, ILLEGAL DRUGS, AND ALCOHOL, JUST TO NAME A FEW. ALWAYS REMEMBER THAT ONE BAD CHOICE COULD CHANGE YOUR LIFE FOREVER! (PAUSE) THINK BEFORE YOU ACT! ALWAYS ASK YOURSELF THIS QUESTION: "HOW WILL THIS CHOICE HELP ME TO BE THE BEST I CAN BE FOR GOD?" (PAUSE)

BEFORE YOU LEAVE THIS SCHOOL, I ENCOURAGE YOU TO MAKE IT A PRIORITY TO PERSONALLY THANK ALL THE PEOPLE THAT HAVE MADE YOUR YEARS HERE PROFITABLE: YOUR PARENTS FOR THE SACRIFICES THEY HAVE MADE FOR YOU TO HAVE A CHRISTIAN EDUCATION AND SHARING THEIR FAITH WITH YOU, YOUR WONDERFUL TEACHERS WHO HAVE BEEN THERE FOR YOU ALL THESE YEARS, AND YOUR CLASSMATES WHO HAVE SHARED THESE YEARS WITH YOU. (PAUSE)

I, MYSELF, THANK GOD FOR ALL THE TIMES I SHARED WITH YOU. I ASK HIM TO BE WITH YOU ON THE REST OF YOUR LIFE'S JOURNEY. LIVE EACH DAY TO THE FULLEST IN SERVING HIM IN ALL YOU DO! MAY GOD CONTINUE TO BLESS EACH OF YOU EVERY DAY WITH HIS LOVE AND I SEND YOU ON YOUR WAY WITH MY LOVE AND BLESSING.

(LET US SPEND A FEW MOMENTS IN SILENT PRAYER.)

DISCUSSION GUIDE

1. NAME SOME OF THE OPPORTUNITIES YOU MIGHT HAVE
   IN HIGH SCHOOL?

> ### POSSIBLE ANSWERS
>
> --retreats
>
> --sports
>
> --different clubs to join
>
> --social activities
>
> --leadership opportunities

2. WHAT ARE SOME OF THE TEMPTATIONS YOU MIGHT
   ENCOUNTER?

3. WHAT SHOULD BE YOUR NUMBER ONE PRIORITY?
   NUMBER TWO? NUMBER THREE?